About Pfeiffer

Pfeiffer serves the professional development and hands-on resource needs of training and human resource practitioners and gives them products to do their jobs better. We deliver proven ideas and solutions from experts in HR development and HR management, and we offer effective and customizable tools to improve workplace performance. From novice to seasoned professional, Pfeiffer is the source you can trust to make yourself and your organization more successful.

Essential Knowledge Pfeiffer produces insightful, practical, and comprehensive materials on topics that matter the most to training and HR professionals. Our Essential Knowledge resources translate the expertise of seasoned professionals into practical, how-to guidance on critical workplace issues and problems. These resources are supported by case studies, worksheets, and job aids and are frequently supplemented with CD-ROMs, websites, and other means of making the content easier to read, understand, and use.

Essential Tools Pfeiffer's Essential Tools resources save time and expense by offering proven, ready-to-use materials—including exercises, activities, games, instruments, and assessments—for use during a training or team-learning event. These resources are frequently offered in looseleaf or CD-ROM format to facilitate copying and customization of the material.

Pfeiffer also recognizes the remarkable power of new technologies in expanding the reach and effectiveness of training. While e-hype has often created whizbang solutions in search of a problem, we are dedicated to bringing convenience and enhancements to proven training solutions. All our e-tools comply with rigorous functionality standards. The most appropriate technology wrapped around essential content yields the perfect solution for today's on-the-go trainers and human resource professionals.

Pfeiffer *Essential resources for training and HR professionals*
www.pfeiffer.com

About This Book

Why is this topic important?

Due to the ever-increasing pace of the world that we live in, the need for equally fast-paced interactive, experiential learning that sticks is continually increasing. Effective learning systems that hold learners' attention and allow them to assimilate information quickly are in high demand, but sadly in short supply. Learn-o-grams™, the picture word logic puzzle book, provides an answer to the demand for accelerated learning in a new and innovative way.

What can you achieve with this book?

Learn-o-grams™ is designed to help teams work together better and to improve their ability to communicate. The game accomplishes this goal by building trust, helping players to carefully manage assumptions and utilize their creative problem-solving abilities. Put another way, this book allows groups to become more open, vulnerable, and alert to others' needs and to practice two-way communication, which improves their listening and feedback skills. By using both their visual and logical intelligences to solve problems, all generations (especially those who like high-energy learning) achieve increased awareness and retention of a wide range of "soft" skills, including communication, teamwork, leadership, and strategic planning. Players also gain understanding of their individual learning styles and cultural differences (diversity) within the team while having a great deal of fun playing this hilarious yet challenging training game.

How is this book organized?

The book itself is divided into three parts. Part One explains the theory behind the game and how it works, its application in the workplace, and how to debrief the game effectively. Part Two is an in-depth explanation of how to play the game and contains detailed instructions. Part Three contains ninety-six black and white picture words with trainers' notes on each picture and on how to explain the logic to players. A CD-ROM accompanies the book. It contains full-color versions of the ninety-six picture words, a scoring sheet, and master answer listings.

Pfeiffer™

Learn-o-grams™

Pictorial Puzzles to Warm Up, Wind Down, and Energize Learning

Ron Roberts

BICENTENNIAL
1807
WILEY
2007
BICENTENNIAL

John Wiley & Sons, Inc.

ISBN-13: 978-0-7879-8682-7

Library of Congress Cataloging-in-Publication Data

Roberts, Ron.
Learn-o-grams : pictorial puzzles to warm up, wind down, and
energize learning / Ron Roberts.
   p. cm.
ISBN-13: 978-0-7879-8682-7 (pbk.)
1. Educational games.   2. Puzzles.   I. Title.
LB1029.G3R63 2007
371.33'7—dc22
                                                                                          2007010537

Acquiring Editor: Martin Delahoussye   Editor: Rebecca Taff
Director of Development: Kathleen Dolan Davies
Production Editor: Dawn Kilgore   Manufacturing Supervisor: Becky Carreño

Printed in the United States of America

Printing   10 9 8 7 6 5 4 3 2 1

Contents

Introduction

WHAT YOU WILL GET FROM LEARN-O-GRAMS™

Learn-o-grams™ is a laugh-out-loud, energizing training program that contains ninety-six picture words, both in print and on a CD-ROM, in four categories: people, places, entertainment, and clichés.

Learn-o-grams™ offers hundreds of different picture/word combinations that allow players to create dozens of different game-play experiences for every audience.

Whether you are a newly formed team with little experience or one of the most sophisticated high-end executive groups, you can enjoy and learn from this game.

WHAT EXACTLY IS A LEARN-O-GRAM™?

A Learn-o-gram™ is simply a combination of words, letters, and mostly pictures that represents a more complex word or phrase.

2

These combinations of pictures and words are all puzzles that you will have to guess by thinking outside the box. Each picture word appears deceptively easy to guess, but usually they are harder than they look, and that is what makes the game so much fun.

• • • • • • • • • • • • • • • • • • • •

WHY LEARN-O-GRAMS™ ARE UNIQUE?

Learn-o-grams™ are so different from any other previous applications of picture words for four basic reasons:

1. Learn-o-grams™ are more sophisticated, complex, and challenging;

2. Each Learn-o-gram™ has been researched for consistency in its ability to convey language so that participants learn from it;

3. All Learn-o-grams™ have been collectively arranged to reach all generations and age ranges. A wide range of picture words from each generation has been placed strategically across the board in order to avoid discriminating against any one group; and

4. Each Learn-o-gram™ has been designed to be humorously entertaining as a stand-alone cartoon. (Our cartoonist has built this feature into every picture word.)

• •

STANDARD AND CUSTOMIZED APPLICATIONS FOR LEARN-O-GRAMS™

This book is truly one of a kind. It can be used to teach and train people from every walk of life in multiple applications, including but not limited to conference and meeting openers, energizers, breaks, topical transitions, and conference closers.

Other applications of the game include teaching about soft skills such as communication, leadership, and risk taking, teamwork and group synergy, strategic planning and execution, process improvement, accelerated learning, and systems thinking.

The Learn-o-gram™ concept is currently being used in corporations, schools, universities, camps, and counseling centers across the United States and appears to have almost unlimited applications. (See Chapter Two for more detail on applications.)

Currently research is in the works for utilizing Learn-o-grams™ in a customized form for very specific and detailed content. For example, we are currently creating a version just for the pharmaceutical industry that uses their specific buzzwords and concepts.

WHY YOU AND YOUR STAFF WILL WANT TO READ THE BOOK

You will want to read this book for several reasons:

1. Most importantly, because *Learn-o-grams*™ combines fun and learning. As we will discuss later, combining fun and learning is essential to increase retention of materials.

2. Merely by playing an innocuous picture word game, readers will have an experiential tool that will help them (or their staff or students) to learn more about how they think and to solve problems.

3. Learn-o-grams™ teach us to think differently. This is one of the only techniques that teaches people, very simply, how to think differently and how to test many of their assumptions. Learn-o-grams™ will help people at all levels of any organization challenge their everyday thinking, as well as many of their preconceived notions about how things ought to be.

4. Learn-o-grams™ will help participants to see their day-to-day events and situations a little more clearly and objectively, instead of through the filter and lenses of their own thinking. Seeing clearly is an advantage in all areas of management, sales, service, and manufacturing.

THE LEARN-O-GRAMS™ STORY

The Learn-o-gram™ pictures are so intense because they are a result of many years of carefully detailed research. The original creator of Learn-o-gram™ was Dr. John Yuscavage, a brilliant pharmacist and inventor from the Wilkes-Barre, Pennsylvania, area who spent about eight years researching and developing this ingenious picture word game.

One day, after talking to John, I received a box in the mail with a crude game board and fifty to seventy-five really cool sample picture word cards, a bunch of dice, a sample game board, and two thirty-six-page clue books. About a quarter of the picture words were designed and hand-drawn in great detail by two very talented artists, James Jiunta and Joe Funaro (who painted the portrait of Clinton at Yale University).

The rest of the picture words were very crudely made out of black-and-white clip art from some type of common software open to the public domain. Some of them were not laid out clearly. Many of them were a little difficult to actually read and understand. There weren't any clues as to what they were, so they were hard to guess unless you looked up the answers in one of the two thirty-page answer books.

This game held great potential, but in its current state it was so complex and the picture words so hard to guess that, after several weeks of evaluating the game, I reluctantly gave up and sent it back, telling John that I wasn't interested.

John—being a very persistent person (and I do not use that term lightly in this case)—would not give up but continued to call me quite frequently to discuss the game in a very professional, polite manner.

● ●

AN INVENTOR'S PERSISTENCE AND INSIGHT FINALLY PAY OFF

There was something fascinating and exciting and almost addictive about those picture words, and I couldn't get them out of my mind. I continued to think about the game for several weeks. I couldn't figure out what I needed to do to make the game work, but I knew it was an incredible game and that all the raw materials were there. It just needed to be polished and refined a little and then we would have the perfect gem.

Having a strong background in the area of communication (I owned a psychological clinic for fifteen years and am currently an adjunct professor of management at Penn State University, Berks), I felt certain that I had the know-how to re-create the cards in a manner that would be fun but challenging—as well as consistent enough to be a valuable learning experience.

The solution was very simple and revolved around the quality and consistency of the artwork. With a few minor alterations, I was sure that we would be able to make this game outstanding.

After pondering the matter late into the wee hours of the night, the next morning, I called John with great excitement and told him to send me just the cards with the picture words on them.

● ●

MAJOR RESEARCH NEEDED, BUT LIGHT AT THE END OF THE TUNNEL

One of the first things our research staff did was to make sure that all the cards had categories printed right on them so that the players would have some idea what they were trying to guess (people, places, entertainment, or clichés). Then our team of outstanding graphic artists, illustrators, and cartoonists went on to finish the job. The team was made up of Clair Poletti, lead artist, and Dave Perillo and Tom Whalen, illustrators and graphic artists.

The research team took over. They set very high standards for the game so that all the artwork would be consistent and easy to understand, and that each picture word would be clear and easily replicated. The team brainstormed weekly and worked very carefully to make sure that we were, in fact, creating a whole new picture word language, which was the key to this game's success.

After a great deal of initial research, we agreed to divide the game into four categories: people, places, entertainment, and clichés. We then discovered that the average person still had problems guessing the answers, so we decided to allow either of two additional options: (1) the person guessing the picture words would receive a series of clues or (2) an entire team of players could use their problem-solving abilities to guess the answers. Option 2 was the most popular solution.

People like learning through games because it combines fun and learning in one fluid model. This is why the game industry continues to thrive and grow. So we carefully worked to help Learn-o-grams™ strike the right balance: to be challenging enough to keep everyone thinking but easy enough so that a large percentage of the participants would, after a bit of hard work, guess the right answer most of the time. We continued to test the game on children in schools, adults at parties, and on my college students.

In fact, some of our best research came as a result of testing the game on my students on the Penn State, Berks, campus. I was teaching organization communication, leadership and motivation, and management at the time, so I had a large contingent of students (referred to as guinea pigs) at my disposal. All the students loved the game, and so did everyone else on whom it was tested. Their feedback made the game better.

GENERATIONAL AND CULTURAL DIFFERENCES RECONCILED

Through our research and constant scrutiny of the game, we discovered one very interesting issue almost by accident: many of the picture words were generation and culture sensitive. We expected that people from different cultures and other countries would have some difficulty solving these problems because English was their second language. We also recognized that many of the names of people and entertainers were very American-centric. However, we were very surprised by the power of generational differences.

We discovered that most players had a basic knowledge about the world that was colored by their generational sunglasses, meaning that each generation knew a whole lot about what happened in their twenty-year compartment or window of growing up, but very little about any other generation's culture and lifestyles, including famous people and entertainers. Even the clichés of the day were different. (The reasons for this are explained in the first chapter.)

Without realizing it, John, the co-inventor, who was in his late fifties, and his artist, who was an octogenarian, were using names and entertainers with whom they were familiar. Lawrence Welk and Richard Burton were great for the older crowd, but not for anyone under thirty.

It was obvious: each generation has different information available to them, they have different technology, and they also have a completely different set of world experiences to which they are exposed.

So we had to go back to the drawing board and make hundreds of new Learn-o-grams™ and sort them to make sure that we had the generation balance required. We then proceeded to put in an equal number of cards from each generation so that every one had the same chance of guessing all the answers correctly.

We also discovered that these simple Learn-o-grams™ actually do transcend language and cultural differences, for the most part. Even people who didn't immediately recognize a Learn-o-grams™ from experience could, after a little practice, guess and decipher the answers because they were learning the universal language of pictures.

● ●

MAKING MAXIMUM USE OF THIS BOOK

So that you can make maximum use of this book, I will explain how the chapters are set up.

In Chapters One and Two, we look at the theory, logic, and psychology behind the design of the game and see how it applies to learning. This part may be especially interesting to those who are in training or teaching.

Chapter Three has material devoted to debriefing any group on what these games teach about making assumptions and the powerful impact that assumptions can have on managing a business, regardless of its product or services.

In Chapter Four, we will take a look at the best method of game play and carefully explain the directions and rules of engagement.

You will find ninety-six picture words (in black and white), with twenty-four of each category (People, Places, Entertainment, and Clichés) and a detailed explanation of (1) the actual Learn-o-gram™ subject; (2) the logic of each picture word and how to solve it; and (3) common misconceptions. Once you review Section Three, you will be able to explain each one of the Learn-o-grams™ during training.

Finally, we provide a full-color CD-ROM from which you can make hundreds of combinations of training warm-ups, starters, topical enhancements, and closers.

Good luck and enjoy the game.

Ron Roberts

The Power of Learn-o-grams™

How and Why They Work!

The History and Theory Behind Learn-o-grams™

LEARN-O-GRAMS™ AND THE REBUS

Learn-o-grams™ have, in one form or another, been around for thousands of years. In fact, all Learn-o-grams™ are simply picture words or what is known as a *rebus*. A rebus is a pictorial representation of any concept, thought, or idea, a grouping of letters, words, pictures, images, and signs (such as + or –) that combine to give a hidden or secret message that has to be decoded. (See examples at the end of this chapter.)

In the caves of early man, there were crude rebus drawings on the walls with representations of events and experiences in their daily lives. The rebus was used by the ancient Egyptians. Their hieroglyphics were an integral part of their daily societal communications. Their engraved picture words still exist today on many of the pyramids in Egypt. It is my understanding that many of the early Native Americans also used the rebus in their leatherwork and art to communicate the deeper meaning in their lives.

In modern times, there are many applications for picture words that tell a story or give specific information. The use of the Rorschach inkblot test in psychology shows how powerful the human mind is in projecting its reality onto even a totally abstract black-and-white inkblot image. Each person who looks at these inkblots sees something different because his or her mind interprets it differently. (This is one of the underpinnings of Learn-o-grams™, called "projection.") Modern businesses use the rebus in a variety of video games and advertising.

Let's take a look at why the rebus is so powerful and why this book can help you to make a difference in your own workplace effectiveness and in your team's performance.

● ●

PICTURES: THE UNIVERSAL LANGUAGE

Why does Hollywood spend billions of dollars each year to create powerful "movies" and television shows that are shown in approximately four thousand theaters and in millions of homes in the United States and the rest of the world?

The answer is simple. The old adage, "A picture is worth a thousand words" has a lot of truth to it. This is also why newspapers and magazines all over the world spend a fortune paying paparazzi for just the right photograph.

Pictures and picture words are the universal language underlying all communication. As we will discuss in later chapters, the mind translates picture words into meaning based on past experiences. To take the value of an image to the extreme, you need go no further than the massive amount of advertising produced to try to influence the buying public with the perfect brand image and just the right photo or drawing.

Businesses spend hundreds of billions of dollars on their brand images. For example, there are the Nike "swoosh" and the NBC peacock. In experiments, even two-year-olds who could barely speak were able to say "Donald's" when they were shown the famous M made of the golden arches.

Show any nationally recognized brand logo to any average person on the street, and a huge number of people will know instantly what product the logo is associated with.

Let's take a look at how these powerful images are applied and see how the Learn-o-grams™ game works.

HOW LEARN-O-GRAMS™ WORKS

Learn-o-grams™ is a fun, exciting, addictive game that allows players to think and learn in an exciting, humorous, pictorial, interactive process. Because Learn-o-grams™ is interactive and experiential, it is different every time it is played. That is why it always evokes such strong emotions. When people play Learn-o-grams™, they usually get to see themselves more clearly and how they as individuals think, learn, and act differently than their colleagues. Each Learn-o-gram™ is a series of very simple word pictures but, because of the complex nature of the human mind, these picture words are often quite difficult to figure out. The human mind, although highly complex, is very predictable and can be tricked quite easily. In order to function effectively, it must figure out which lines of logic to apply to solve a given problem. The mind works best when it has an experience to relate back to or a baseline of past activity to reference.

The Learn-o-grams™ game consistently challenges players' minds to figure out the logic behind a picture word. (You can learn more about this in Chapters Three and Four.) The average player will find that some puzzles are easy and that some are hard. There is no way to predict which ones will be hard or easy because it is all based on each individual's perceptual abilities and his or her particular body of experience.

THE GAME WHERE LEARNING IS FUN

One thing that every player will experience is lots of fun, fun, fun. Every time any individual or group tries to guess a picture word and gets the answer right, the entire team laughs out loud, cheers, and becomes more addicted (and can't wait to do the next one to demonstrate their newfound expertise).

However, when a team doesn't guess correctly, there is always a very loud moaning sound (sort of like the echo of a fully grown moose in the distant mountains) emitted by the player or group and a definitive crying of "Arghhh."

The reason for this is because the answer is always totally obvious once the players hear someone say it. Again, because of the nature of the human mind, the answer often evades detection. Once the participants see the simple logic behind an answer, most people say out loud, "I can't believe I didn't see that" or "The answer was right in front of me." (See Chapter Four for more details on the human mind and Learn-o-grams™.)

LEARN-O-GRAMS™ CREATES INTENSE, LONG-LASTING LEARNING

Not only is Learn-o-grams™ fun, but it a powerful teaching tool. Playing the game creates incredibly strong emotions. Any time you combine strong emotions with learning, the intensity and retention of the learning experience are increased dramatically.

Retention is increased because the emotions of the moment are attached to the learning and thus embedded deep in the subconscious.

ANALYSIS OF A FEW LEARN-O-GRAMS™

Following is a practical outline of how to interpret and guess a Learn-o-gram™. In order to give you a comprehensive understanding of how to solve these picture word puzzles, we show one easy sample from each of the four categories of Learn-o-grams™ in the game.

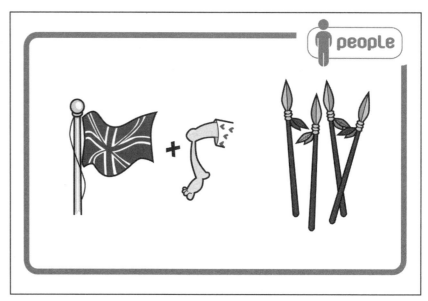

(Brit + Knee + Spears)

This picture word is classified as "People," which means it is a famous person. A British flag is followed by a plus sign and someone's leg, bent at the knee. Then there is a bunch of spears. So you would have British-Leg-Spears. But the plus sign means the first two words are one unit. We also know that this is a famous person. So we run through our minds, "British + leg" and "spears" over and over again. Suddenly the light goes on. We know a famous person with the last name of Spears. So then our mind's ability to process a part of the picture and get the whole concept (also known to psychologists as part-to-whole logic) kicks in and we see that it is Brit + knee (a part of the leg) Spears or Britney Spears. The amazing thing is that all this logic can happen in your brain in just a split second.

First, it is important to note that this rebus is of a Place, that is, a city, state, or country. Above we see an old-fashioned washboard and a 2,000-pound weight. This can be simplified into "washing" and "weight." But the mind is so fast that it recognizes that the 2,000 pounds is not just a weight but it is also a "ton." Then you use your part-to-whole logic to figure out that it is "washing" plus "ton" or Washington.

This picture word is based around a famous TV show or movie title. Knowing this will help our minds to sort through the numerous possible solutions and be more selective. First, we see a bunch of numbers that are different colors. Next, we see a coffee cup with the letter "L" on it. So, without any additional input, it would read "colored numbers" and then a separate word "L coffee cup."

Upon further analysis, we could also note that the numbers are all odd numbers. We could also look at the cup and see a combination of L and coffee cup in reversed order as "coffee cup L." So we could put together, in our minds, the combination of "odd numbers" and "coffee cup L."

If you happen to be a little older, this may start to ring a bell. If not, you are left to sound out the name. Eventually, you would come up with "odd" "cup L" or "odd couple" or "The Odd Couple," a famous movie from more than twenty years ago.

This category, Clichés, is the most difficult because they are so abstract. This Learn-o-gram™ shows a picture of a sink, a paddle, and the left arm of someone swimming. So it might mean, "sink," "paddle," "one-armed swimmer." Or if you let your miraculous mind go to work and try and figure out the larger picture from the smaller parts, you might also see "sink" "oar" "swim." Suddenly, the light goes on and the answer is actually an old saying, "Sink or swim." Congratulations on a job well done.

So now you have an idea not only of what a Learn-o-gram™ is, but also how the game works in general game play.

Since you have a general grasp of what is going on in the Learn-o-grams™ game, let's look at some of their applications and how they tie back to the workplace and various educational settings in Chapter Two.

A Game with Multiple Applications

● ● ● ● ● ● ● ● ● ● ● ● ● ● ● ● ● ● ● ●

AN APPLICATION FOR EVERY OCCASION

The Learn-o-grams™ game offers a variety of applications and can be adapted in many different ways in the workplace and in the classroom. In the fast-paced business world today, learning must occur more and more quickly in order to keep up with rapid change. With ever-increasing international competition and technological change, the ability for workers and students alike to assimilate information takes on greater urgency.

The Learn-o-grams™ game helps players to do this through playing the game itself, which teaches them how to process information.

Many of those who are trying to assimilate new knowledge today are much more sophisticated and demanding than in the past. The increased demand occurs because learners are surrounded by and inundated with high-speed technology—the Internet, video games, and lightning-fast computers—from a very early age. Because of this early conditioning, today's learners require a faster pace of education. Learning must occur in quick, clear, smaller blocks to be effective. In order to cope with this requirement, instructors and trainers are being forced to "experientialize" a large portion of their training. The bar has been raised substantially so that successful, meaningful training must not only be rich in content but also challenging, interactive, and experiential, as well as fun and exciting.

In order to meet the needs of the modern short-attention-span information-seeker, today's instructors must also teach in small, high-energy, experiential, interactive modules. The concept of "edutainment" (combining education and entertainment) has spread to nearly every corner of the corporate world and has almost become standard as a teaching techniques.

Imparting knowledge requires that learners pay attention, assimilate, and comprehend the material. This requires the constant release of energy. Energy, it turns out, is the modern instructor's key to success. Learners get energy from experiential exercises, from interactive connections, and from having fun and laughing during training. Learn-o-grams™ help today's complex learners by freeing up their very valuable psychic energy.

● ● ● ● ● ● ● ● ● ● ● ● ● ● ● ● ● ● ● ●

FOUR POWERFUL APPLICATIONS

The great news is that the Learn-o-grams™ game meets many of the learners' needs through four major applications: chronological, organizational, observational, and soft skill learning.

1. *Chronological applications.* Learn-o-grams™ can be applied at certain key times throughout training in order to energize and motivate participants.

2. *Organizational applications.* Learn-o-grams™ can be applied within an organization at various levels, such as executive, management, supervisory, line staff, sales, or customer service, to increase the overall system's awareness of various processes.

3. *Observational applications.* Learning can be said to have occurred when an outside observer is able to make certain inferences about how a group performs during an experience or task. Learn-o-grams™ assists in this process.

4. *Soft-skill applications.* Learn-o-grams™ can be applied to help improve soft skills and process management.

The following is a more in-depth look at the four applications.

Chronological Applications

In any conference, meeting, or gathering, formal or informal, certain transitions naturally occur. It has become more and more common to have some form of "edutainment" presented during these transitions. A key feature of Learn-o-gram™ games is the high degree of flexibility in how they can be used. Here are some great ways to apply Learn-o-grams™ throughout any event.

Openers and Icebreakers

Every organization wants to impress its members. In today's fast-paced, high-pressure business world, it is important to have a way to get people to relax, warm up, and—most importantly—open up. A small investment in an opener or an icebreaker will likely be paid back very quickly in the form of increased creativity, greater focus on the situation at hand, and uplifted morale and motivation.

Energizers, Breaks, and Intermissions

Today's students become bored very easily, and instructors have to work doubly hard to maintain their attention. The best way to keep attention at a high level is to balance the less interesting factual materials with breaks and energizers to keep learners' batteries recharged. The boost that comes from even one good energizer can increase receptivity, alertness, and retention dramatically.

Closers

There is an old saying, "Always leave them laughing." What's a better way to close any event or conference than with the positive energy of laughter? The Learn-o-gram™ game gives the audience the opportunity to laugh out loud while enjoying the power of learning.

When people are laughing, they are creating strong positive emotions that I believe create powerful neuro-associative conditioning anchors, which allow learning to be deeply embedded and retained.

ORGANIZATIONAL APPLICATIONS

There is a major need at every organizational level for employees to learn and expand their horizons. How valuable is the ability to think progressively and differently in the workplace? The answer is simple and obvious: it is the lifeblood of future success in every aspect of the corporate world today. In meetings I have held as a consultant for dozens of executives at Fortune 500 companies, there is a severe dearth of progressive, forward, open thinking and creativity. Every field of endeavor needs new ideas and breakthrough thinking to go to the next level. Let's take a quick look at a few of the implications for Learn-o-grams™ by area within an organization.

After each description of an application of Learn-o-grams™, I will indicate the positive effects of a healthy or the negative effects of a fixed mental model for a person at that level of the organization.

By way of explanation, a "mental model" is how any person thinks and how he or she imposes his or her thinking (whether limiting or freeing up) on others and on the task at hand. How you manage your own mental model greatly affects your performance and the performance of your team.

Executive Applications

Visioning is of the utmost importance for executives in today's highly competitive international marketplace. Vision drives the executive's ability to transform his or her entire organization. Every great leader must have the ability to see things in a different light, to create new direction and strategies for his or her organization, and to implement his or her ideas.

There is an old saying, "Without vision, my people perish." That saying is as true today as it was thousands of years ago when it was used in the Old Testament.

- *Mental Model for an Executive.* Every executive must be able to communicate a philosophy and implement his or her decisions within an organization. Whether the executive has a fixed perspective and rigidly adheres to the status quo or whether he or she

is open to change and fresh new ideas, a new vision, and transforming concepts can make the difference between success and mediocrity.

- *How Learn-o-grams™ Can Help Executives Achieve Their Goals.* In combination with other training tools, Learn-o-grams™ can give senior managers a new awareness of what is possible (seeing things anew), offer them a place to take some small risks, and help them to be more open to their peers and colleagues.

- *Example of an Executive Application.* In working with a group of about fifteen C-level movie executives from a very successful, rapidly growing, publicly traded, cutting-edge, high-tech company in Las Vegas, we used the Learn-o-grams™ game. The results were fascinating. All of these very powerful men and woman secretly thought they knew it all. Once they faltered and floundered when solving simple picture word puzzles, we showed them that that these same strong preconceived notions that had prevented them from succeeding in the game were, in fact, the same types of preconceived notions that prevented them from operating their large company efficiently. They all began to discuss the fact that many of their own limiting factors were self-imposed. The result was greatly increased openness and interest in thinking more freely.

Management and Supervisor Applications

Managers and supervisors want to help fulfill their leader's ultimate objective of growing the company. To do this, they must think creatively and "outside the box" to improve performance and increase efficiency while motivating people to the max. Whether utilizing strategic or tactical thinking or applying creative problem solving and group brainstorming, all managers and supervisors must try to manage change and improve their own performance and the performance of their subordinates.

- *Mental Model for Managers and Supervisors.* Great managers must think differently in every area for which they are responsible and help colleagues and subordinates tap into their creativity to achieve success for the whole team. If the manager doesn't do his or her job, the whole team will falter in its attempts to achieve its objectives.

- *How Learn-o-grams™ Can Help.* Learn-o-grams™ helps management to sync up and be "on the same page." This game also helps management and supervisors to realize that, to succeed, they have to think at higher levels of creativity and ingenuity and work together within the organizational system.

- *Example for Managers and Supervisors.* A group of fifteen plant managers from a large electric generation plant was in a comprehensive partnership with a large engineering group for a three-year period to retrofit their plant to meet new government regulations for clean air. This was to be an almost billion-dollar renovation.

After we used the Learn-o-grams™ game as part of a final debriefing on their training in communication, they realized two significant things: (1) because they were all part of the same system, in order to achieve their objectives of being on time and on budget, they would have to be on the same page in terms of understanding their objective and what steps they would take to carry it out, and (2) they would have to be open to new ways of thinking and solving problems, just as in Learn-o-grams™. They could not let their preconceived notions of what was expected keep them from pushing the project to a higher level.

Sales

Seeing new value or new applications for a product or service (and convincing others they need it) is the secret of successful salespeople all over the world. Seeing the possibility of achieving goals beyond the norm is key and a vital part of any sales effort. Going beyond what seems possible is the differentiator between a good salesperson and a great sales entrepreneur.

- *Mental Models for Sales.* A fixed mental model will prevent a salesperson from achieving a higher sales quota or going beyond his or her objectives. Creative thinking means no limits, and a salesperson with this kind of mental model will achieve outstanding results.

- *How Learn-o-grams™ Helps.* Using Learn-o-grams™ helps sales teams to create an open culture of trust. It also helps teams to define their culture and determine who the competition really is—the external competition, not the other teams within their organization.

- *Example for Sales.* A team of food manufacturing salespeople I worked with viewed Learn-o-grams™ as part of their training. After seeing the game, they realized the power of sharing information within their group and how difficult it had been for them to takes risks and admit possibly making a mistake. After this training, a group of salespeople admitted to holding back vital information from other teams in order to beat them. As we discussed this problem, they admitted that it was because of the competition to be number one within the organization. We then discussed the deadly power of internal competition. We also discussed the importance of having an open culture similar to the one that they created when playing a successful game of Learn-o-grams™. Both of the teams experienced a 15 percent jump in their numbers within three months after the training.

Customer Service

Reframing or seeing situations and problems from the customer's point of view and from a different perspective is essential to grow any company. Seeing the situation from the perspective of the customer and being able to fix problems quickly can make or break a company. If a company does not understand what motivates and satisfies its customers, even the best company can lose new sales and, worse still, repeat customers.

- *Mental Model for Customer Service.* Your mental model and its flexibility will make the difference between great and mediocre customer service and can affect your entire organization and its future growth.

- *How Learn-o-grams™ Helps.* By understanding the logic behind each solution to the puzzle and figuring out how to apply them, customer service representatives (CSRs) can learn to break down their clients' actions into smaller, more logical, orderly segments. Once the CSR is dealing with smaller segments, he or she will have more success and a better outcome from each customer contact.

- *Example for Customer Service*: A group of CSRs from a large telemarketing company was able to learn different ways of reframing their customers' negative and angry actions after playing the Learn-o-grams™ game and realizing the parallels between their work and the game. By learning to relax when overwhelmed in the middle of the Learn-o-grams™ game, the CSRs were able to relax and be more objective when helping their clients, instead of taking customers' reactions personally.

● ●

OBSERVATIONAL APPLICATIONS

Learn-o-grams™ helps trainers by allowing them to observe raw behavior as it occurs during game play. Here are a few of the types of observation that can be made by watching participants play the game. Observations made during the game are especially valuable for managers, supervisors, HR staff, and others who want to remain relatively detached and neutral.

The following paragraphs describe some key areas that can be observed and give some examples.

Learning Styles: Auditory, Visual, and Tactile Patterns

How we learn is vitally important to how quickly we assimilate information and how well we manage a new situation. The game is highly visual in nature, and thus visual learners may perform better than average. But this fact does not diminish the valuable role of auditory (hearing) and tactile (hands-on) learners within a team.

Although these types of learners often struggle initially, they can add great value in the overall success of any session.

- *Example from an Actual Learn-o-grams™ Game.* One player on the team happened to be a visual learner. He easily found several of the answers, but was totally stumped by one Learn-o-gram™. Try as he might, neither he nor his team members could solve it. Finally, one of the auditory learners on the team threw her head down in frustration. The visual learner kept repeating the parts of the Learn-o-gram™ out loud in a disjointed manner. Droning on, he repeated them over and over. To her surprise, the auditory learner heard the visually astute player saying the incorrect answer over and over again. Just then, the light went on and in a split second, she could hear the answer in the stuttering of the visual learner, even though her head was on the table and she had her eyes shut. She sat up and solved the puzzle immediately.

- *Observational Value.* Supervisors and managers and even colleagues can observe others in their attempts to solve the puzzles and discuss how learning styles affect performance back at the workplace. This is a perfect setting to help players see their own strengths and weaknesses based on their learning styles and see how seamlessly they all can work together.

Control Issues: Parent, Adult, Child Ego States

According to transactional analysis theory, within every person there are Parent, Adult, and Child ego states. Usually one of these states is more active than the others. If a person is comfortable operating in any of the three states and able to move easily from one to the next depending on the demands of the moment, he or she will be more successful in dealing with others.

Unfortunately, most people are not even aware of what state they favor. How a participant plays the game can demonstrate his or her ego state quite clearly. Let's take a look at what each ego state would look like.

- *Observational Value for Parent Ego State.* Usually, those with an over-active Parent ego state will be controlling and try to lead the team to solve the problem by themselves—or at least be the primary force in orchestrating the process.

- *Observational Value for Adult Ego State.* Those with a more highly developed Adult ego state will be more analytical and logical and will be most helpful keeping everyone on track and correcting anyone who errs in judgment. The Adult ego state is not as critical as the Parent ego state nor as creative as the Child ego state.

- *Observational Value for Child Ego State.* Those with an active Child ego state may be the most creative and spontaneous in solving the picture word puzzles but

may need the assistance of someone with a Parent or Adult ego state to stay focused.

Trust and Openness

Trust is an essential foundation for all communication. The degree to which players trust one another in their teams will show in their ability to take risks and make mistakes. If the team displays a culture of openness and trust, then mistakes and errors will be accepted openly and can lead to greater innovation and creativity.

- *Observational Value.* Watching the team to see how they handle it when a colleague makes a mistake or gives the wrong answer will give clues about the level of trust and openness on a team. The culture of the team and its level of openness to innovation and new ideas may also become readily apparent.

- *Overall Observational Example.* A senior-level manager came to observe a training program with Learn-o-grams™ to find possible future leaders as part of her succession planning program to promote the best and the brightest. She was able to observe participants in a neutral, low-key, non-threatening setting. She was shocked to discover several very talented potential leaders whom she previously thought were more average in nature. It is not uncommon for new talent to surface during a training session. The reason why is simple: many participants take more risks and lose many of the inhibitions that previously held them back when in the safety and comfort of a "fun," innocuous team-building game.

● ●

SOFT-SKILLS APPLICATIONS

Learn-o-grams™ can be used to teach and debrief about many of the soft skills that enhance learning. These include but are not limited to the following:

Communication   Strategic planning

Teamwork   Execution

Leadership   Process improvement

Risk taking   Systems thinking

Soft skills help participants to manage tasks and process new methods for improving them. The Learn-o-grams™ game can improve many of these skills just through playing it. Soft skills are covered more thoroughly in the next chapter.

Diversity Training

Interestingly, Learn-o-grams™ has a clear correlation to training in the area of diversity, which here refers to the diversity of thinking and talent within any organization. Diversity in this sense is really all about two different key areas:

1. Managing assumptions about other people or controlling our preconceived notions about what we expect from them, and

2. Thinking differently ourselves and having a tolerance for such different thinking in others.

Learn-o-grams™ addresses both of these areas. By playing the game, we can learn to challenge many of our basic assumptions about how we communicate. We can also take a look at many of our preconceived notions as the game unfolds and generalize back to the work setting during the debriefing. More tangentially, playing Learn-o-grams™ allows participants to discuss the type of culture in their organization and their openness to different ways of thinking.

CUSTOMIZED AND SPECIALIZED CONTENT APPLICATIONS

This section is focused on ways to create your own customized Learn-o-grams™ based on specialized content in your organization.

This is a very important application because every business has a special vocabulary, technical know-how and descriptions, and product-related information. Some of these products and services can be so complicated or have such long, dry standard operating procedures (SOPs) that they are difficult to learn and retain.

By creating your own custom Learn-o-gram™, you can improve learning and retention dramatically in your training programs.

Some examples follow.

- A large pharmaceutical company I was consulting with wanted us to help them improve their process of instructing and communicating their lengthy, tedious standard operating procedures for several of their more complicated pharmaceutical products. This was a perfect application, and the Learn-o-grams™ provided powerful anchors for improving training and retention while creating powerful energizing breaks.

- Another related application was for one of the nation's largest pharmaceutical magazines. They are in the process of adding a Learn-o-gram™ per month to their magazine to create a more fun and exciting brand image.

- Several other organizations have taken on the task of creating Learn-o-grams™ for their divisions or teams that will be their symbols of success. This is an unusual application, but it seems to be very popular because it creates a visual icon and improves morale.

As can be seen, Learn-o-grams™ truly has multiple applications in the workplace. How you choose to customize your program will be based on the needs of your organization. In my experience, the unique mix of fun, cartoon-like graphics and the serious learning aspects of the Learn-o-grams™ game allows participants to achieve incredible learning objectives.

In the next chapter we will discuss the art of debriefing Learn-o-grams™ and see just how some companies are using this game to maximize learning.

Learn-o-grams™ in the Workplace

● ●

LEARN-O-GRAMS™ TEACH SOFT SKILLS EXPERIENTIALLY

One of the amazing aspects of the Learn-o-grams™ game is that it teaches all sorts of soft skills just through the experience of playing the game. Soft skills include, but are not limited to, communication, teamwork, leadership, strategic planning and execution, process improvement,

and change management. Communication skills improve the ability to work together. Teamwork helps people do tasks. Leadership and motivation help leaders involve others.

The reason soft skills are so hard to learn is because we can only learn them through actual experience and trial and error. Very few employees want to walk up to their bosses or co-workers and say, "Hey, I was wondering if I might try out some new out-of-the-box communication skills on you. In order to do this, I will probably be very uncomfortable and act really strange for a few minutes. Do you mind?" The boss might say you were crazy and probably not think too highly of you after that.

Your compassionate comrades would think you were completely off the wall if you asked them to join you in this high-risk-taking activity. Of course, if it goes well in your practice session, you could receive great accolades and probably a promotion for your effort, but if you perform poorly, you are at risk of being fired.

Most people never get to improve their soft skills because it is too scary and risky, or they just never find a place that is safe enough to practice. That being said, Learn-o-grams™ uses the safety of an experiential learning game to teach very important but often neglected soft skills.

● ●

SOFT SKILLS DRIVE HARD SKILLS

From observing hundreds of companies and thousands of employees, managers, and executives over the past sixteen years, I have decided that soft skills drive hard skills. The ability to manage soft skills will deeply affect your ability to carry out the tasks you try to achieve each and every day.

Whether you are a doctor, a lawyer, a manufacturing plant assembler, a middle-level manager, or a clerk in a department store, the same truth applies: soft skills drive hard skills. The ability to perform any task, build any product, initiate any service, all require soft skills and the ability to interact with people.

Because people are so important to any process, soft skills are especially important. Because nothing happens without people, those who are most proficient at soft skills will be promoted and win every time, unless you work in a totally computerized or robotic setting—and even then you had better hope that there are some people around to repair the computers and robots.

What does all this have to do with Learn-o-grams™? The Learn-o-grams™ game helps to sensitize participants to the more subtle side of communication simply by playing the game. With the help of a good trainer, Learn-o-grams™ will allow participants to observe themselves (and their behaviors) while playing the game. Let's look at a paradigm of soft skills that I have developed through thousands of hours of painstaking observation.

Figure 3.1 shows how soft skills are developed and maintained. This paradigm shows that communication is at the center of all successful endeavors.

In the soft skills ladder, *communication* is at the center because it is key to all success. Communication has as its foundation two key features: *trust* and *assumptions*. Trust often waxes and wanes, depending on how your relationships evolve. Ideally, however, *trust* grows as people of good standing continue to be responsible and demonstrate their reliability and integrity. As trust grows, so does the level of communication in a relationship. Our *assumptions* come

SOFT SKILLS LADDER PARADIGM

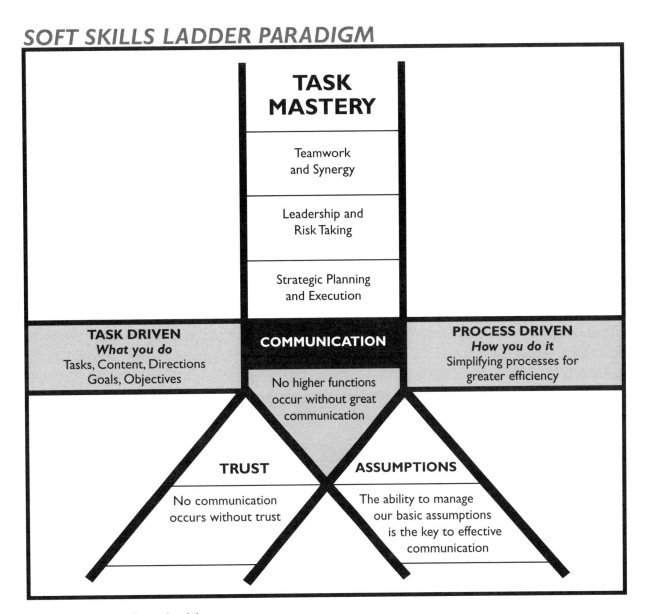

FIGURE 3.1   The Soft Skill Paradigm Ladder

from the ways in which we perceive situations and experiences. All of our past experiences and future expectations are a filter through which we see life.

All *tasks* (*what* we do) and the subsequent mastery of these tasks require superior communication. The building blocks of task mastery are *teamwork and synergy, leadership and risk taking,* and *strategic planning and execution.* Our success in completing tasks is based on our ability to communicate the processes (*how* we do tasks) to others.

Learn-o-grams™ is such an effective tool because playing the game helps us build trust in others and improves our ability to manage assumptions (the foundations of good communication). While playing the game, we must use good communication, which results in our practicing teamwork, leadership, and risk taking in a safe, non-threatening environment.

All portions of the ladder must be in harmony (from the bottom rung to the top) in order for us to gain greater mastery over any task and to demonstrate process improvement and performance efficiency.

● ●

DEBRIEFING LEARN-O-GRAMS™

All debriefing invokes feedback—both positive and negative—on how any individual or team has performed a task. Debriefing an experience is very important in order to achieve continual improvement. There are two key elements to most debriefings:

1. Discussion and questions with everyone in the group about *what* they did, and

2. More feedback and discussion about *how* they achieved their results or the process they used to accomplish the goal.

As we mentioned, Learn-o-grams™ have an incredible ability to teach soft skills such as communication, teamwork, leadership, and process improvement, and debriefing the experience greatly influences the retention of such learning. The debriefing can be very powerful, as it is based on behavior that everyone in the group has just observed.

The Learn-o-grams™ game can be debriefed in either of two ways:

● Participants can discuss certain topical or content-based learning that occurs directly as a result of playing the game, or

● A facilitator can lead a discussion on how the participants felt during the game and look closely at each player's choices and reactions, leading to personal insights.

Use the following points when debriefing the Learn-o-grams™ experience, based on the learning areas you want to emphasize.

Communication

Key concept. To excel at Learn-o-grams™ or any other task, you must be a stellar communicator.

PROCESS POINTS

- To succeed in solving the Learn-o-grams™, each player must be able and willing to communicate loud and clear with the other players on the team.

- Unless there is intense, straightforward, open communication, the puzzles may remain beyond the scope of any one person to solve easily. By merely saying the answers that you think are best for each puzzle, you may help your fellow team players to solve them.

- Each card has a big picture composed of several smaller pictures. To the degree that you communicate all of what you actually see out loud to your team, your teammates are better able to achieve victory.

BACK TO THE WORKPLACE

- Communication is the key to achievement in the workplace.

- Being assertive and proactive and communicating effectively, combined with the ability to see the big picture, is always a winning strategy.

Managing Assumptions

Key concept. To the degree that you actively manage your assumptions, you will have a better grasp on reality and achieve more accurate results in Learn-o-grams™ or on the job.

PROCESS POINTS

- Managing one's assumptions is much more complex than it would appear. In the Learn-o-grams™ game, wrong assumptions abound. Understanding the logic of each piece of the picture and determining the rules by which one makes assumptions is essential to success in Learn-o-grams™ and in life. Attempting to understand and discern the type of logic used in each segment of the picture will increase your number of correct answers.

- We make thousands of assumptions every day in the work setting, and it is very easy to make a few wrong ones. By learning to manage our assumptions, we increase our effectiveness in the area of communication and thus become more efficient in all the higher-level task-based skills such as teamwork, leadership, and strategic planning.

BACK TO THE WORKPLACE

- If we do not manage our assumptions carefully, we will start to build our plans on a foundation that either does not fit our needs or that is literally sitting on quicksand. Either way, all of our good work may either have to be redone at great time and/or expense to the company or, worse yet, may fail completely. Managing our assumptions is one of the most important underpinnings of all soft skills.

Leadership and Risk Taking

Key concepts. One of the most difficult parts of being a leader is taking risks. If you are a success, you are the hero. If you perform at less than a desirable level, you are still accountable for the entire performance.

PROCESS POINTS

- In order to play Learn-o-grams™ successfully and to really increase their ability at solving the puzzles,

players must take risks. Giving the wrong answer as you struggle is an important step toward figuring out the logic in the puzzle. (Most people just sit there looking at the picture word puzzle silently suffering, without a clue of the answer.)

- Speaking out takes courage. Only a true leader will have the courage to be the first one to say the wrong answer. This type of behavior will help others on the team to succeed.

- Opening up and sharing our ideas with the rest of the team is no small task. To succeed at Learn-o-grams™ it is necessary to open up, take a chance, and risk performing less that perfectly.

BACK TO THE WORKPLACE

- The ability to take a qualified risk is rare among workers. All great leaders have this quality. To what extent do you or your team take qualified risks in the workplace?

Trust

Key concepts. To take risks, there must be trust. For us to trust one another, the culture we work in must support that trust.

PROCESS POINTS

- Only when team members trust each other will they open up and take greater risks.

- It takes tremendous trust in your fellow teammates to be the one who gives a wrong answer in order to jump-start the team and improve performance. Only through trusting another can you have the courage to say whatever comes to mind and know that you will not be laughed at, made fun of, or rejected.

- Trust allows the group to work with greater cohesiveness and unity. Trusting each other in the little things can, over time, generalize into a culture of trust throughout an organization.

BACK TO THE WORKPLACE

- What kind of culture exists at your workplace in the area of trust? What can you do to improve that culture? How can you find ways to address this need openly and discuss the need for greater trust and the effects that this will have on performance?

Teamwork and Synergy

Key concepts. Only when a team coalesces and is in real unity will it attain the synergy necessary to achieve greatness in both Learn-o-grams™ and the workplace.

PROCESS POINTS

- The ability for a team to work together and coalesce is one of the most important components of success in the Learn-o-grams™ game and in the workplace.

- "Two heads are better than one" is true. The collective abilities of the group are much more powerful for solving the puzzles than the talents of any one individual. The more difficult Learn-o-grams™ puzzles demand peak group performance in order to solve them.

BACK TO THE WORKPLACE

- The need for teamwork is no longer disputed, but there always seems to be room for improvement in the level of commitment that players demonstrate. Playing Learn-o-grams™ can help improve this level of commitment because all members have to work together to succeed.

Process Improvement and Accelerated Learning

Key concepts. Constant process improvement and acceleration of learning are necessary to stay competitive and win in Learn-o-grams™ and in today's workplace.

PROCESS POINTS

- Mastering Learn-o-grams™ requires that participants learn as they go about the process of attempting to solve the puzzles. By understanding the *process* of solving the puzzles (a new language, logic, and rules), players can improve their problem-solving ability and be at the top of their game.

- Accelerating learning is merely the act of gaining mastery over the processes involved in any task.

BACK TO THE WORKPLACE

- Continually improving processes and accelerating your ability to learn is not only necessary to succeed in Learn-o-grams™ but also important for managing the constant change that occurs in the business world.

Strategic Planning and Execution

Key concepts. Although taking the time to plan strategically at the beginning of a process slows you down a little, it will dramatically improve performance over the long run.

PROCESS POINTS

- A simple plan for how to attack each new Learn-o-grams™ puzzle is necessary to perform well in the game. Having a team strategy early in the game is a great advantage.

- Because each Learn-o-gram™ has a different logic component to it, it is necessary for teams to decipher these logic patterns. Once it figures out the patterns, a team's performance will improve considerably.

BACK TO THE WORKPLACE

- The ability to plan strategically and execute well apply both to the Learn-o-grams™ game and to almost every aspect of the real work world.

Creative Problem Solving and Diversity of Thinking

Key concepts. The ability to think differently, be creative, and be innovative is in short supply in the corporate world. To the degree to which you gain mastery over these through playing Learn-o-grams™, your ability to manage difficult and complex problems and situations increases dramatically. Embracing differences and diversity is the secret to success for your team in solving complex problems.

PROCESS POINTS

- The power of creative problem solving and diversity is at the center of the Learn-o-grams™ game. In order to do well at the game, participants must either have an innate ability to think creatively or they must develop their ability to think outside of the box and to rely on the natural diversity of their teams.

- Most participants do not naturally have this ability, so Learn-o-grams™ is a useful tool for helping players to gain a greater awareness of how to tap into the diversity of talent on their teams.

- As players gain skills at the game and learn to depend on their teammates, utilizing group brainstorming more often, their creative problem-solving ability naturally gets better.

- Diversity includes regional and geographical differences that players can actually experience through play. For example, the word "soda" might be called "pop" or "tonic" in another area of the country.

BACK TO THE WORKPLACE

- The ability to be creative and think differently is one of the greatest gifts that any individual can offer in the workplace. Embracing the diversity of thinking on any team and generating creative solutions are important for any team.

Systems Thinking

Key concepts. Every action that any individual or team makes will dramatically affect the whole system eventually.

PROCESS POINTS

- Because the logic behind a Learn-o-gram™ is seldom obvious at first glance (by design), it is often necessary to look at each component of the picture word in a larger context to solve the puzzle. Only by seeing each item as a part of the system for which it was constructed can any player or team grasp the full meaning of that Learn-o-gram™.

- Seeing the broader scope in order to understand the impact of any action on the system is also very relevant to applications in business.

BACK TO THE WORKPLACE

- When individuals or teams become sensitized to the impact that their individual actions have on the larger system, the system becomes more harmonious and synchronized, and often experiences radical improvements in productivity.

● ●

OBSERVATIONAL DEBRIEFINGS

Observing learning patterns, behaviors, and reactions that occur during actual game play can be enlightening to most observers and to the players themselves. Simply watching the play of the game can bring new levels of insight and real-time awareness about how individuals behave and how they act as a team.

In the following paragraphs are some observational questions that you can ask to debrief at a deeper level during the short interval debriefing breaks between game play of Learn-o-grams™.

COMMUNICATION

1. Is your communication more efficient if you talk to each other?

2. Why don't people talk to each other during the first round?

3. What is the impact of increased communication on your problem-solving ability?

4. How much more efficient is your communication if you give each other feedback during game play?

5. What is the difference between one-way and two-way communication? What does this difference mean for the game? How does this difference impact your organization?

Interpretation of Answers. You will be able to glean the team's level of communication based on the depth of answers that they give. Encourage the participants to dig deeper into why their level of communication is in the state that it is. You may also want to give them an assignment to practice a new form of two-way communication or some other new task and ask them to report back to their supervisor or to you at a pre-set time (one week or thirty days).

TEAMWORK AND SYNERGY

1. Did you work as a team?

2. To what extent did your team openly give feedback to each other?

3. Did you share best practices or did you guard your own turf?

4. At any time, did the small teams go to any other outside teams for help?

Interpretation of Answers. Depending on how the team responds, you can see very quickly whether you are working with a cohesive or a diffused team. Push deeper to see whether they are able to share information or whether they, like most groups, are careful with—and even hoard—information. Information is the second-most valuable commodity that any team has. People are obviously still number one.

LEADERSHIP AND RISK TAKING

1. Who took the most risks?

2. What was the effect of this increased risk taking on overall performance?

3. Who was willing to make a mistake or say the wrong thing and be different? What was the effect?

4. How does a player's level of authority in the workplace affect his or her performance on this task?

Interpretation of Answers. By looking at the answers you receive here, you can assess whether this is a risk-taking group or a cautious, risk-aversive group. You can inquire which of the two types of leadership they have attained: *positional authority* (assigned by a higher-ranking official) or *ascribed authority* (rank earned because of the respect of others and a natural gift of leadership).

STRATEGIC PLANNING AND EXECUTION

1. When guessing the answers, did your team come up with a working plan or just shoot from the hip without planning?

2. Did your team take a *tactical* (taking sequential steps in an orderly fashion to solve puzzles) or a *strategic* (evaluating the goal and figuring out the best way to get there) approach to planning? Why?

Interpretation of Answers. Whether a team plans tactically or strategically will make all the difference in its performance. As they develop a format for managing to solve problems with the game puzzles, they may also become more clear about planning in the workplace. Find out their approach and see whether it is reflective of how they manage and plan in the workplace.

PROCESS IMPROVEMENT

1. Did your team continually think of new ways to improve the process and become efficient at solving the puzzles?

2. If and when the initial plan did not work, how long did it take your team to change direction?

3. Did team members blame each other or try to fix the process?

4. Did your team have to resort to a contingency plan due to process breakdown at any time? If so, how did it manage to change course?

Interpretation of Answers. A team's ability to think on its feet and change on the fly can make the difference between success and mediocrity. Drilling a little more deeply into the area of process improvement will help you to see how teams manage when everything doesn't go perfectly (which in truth is most of the time). Understanding their ability to manage processes and know whether they need to work on this area will help them greatly to improve performance.

CREATIVE PROBLEM SOLVING

1. What was the effect of group brainstorming on performance?

2. What happened when your team started bouncing thoughts off one another?

3. Were you able at any time to tap into your "stream of creativity"?

Interpretation of Answers. Knowing the level of creativity of your team is critical in the workplace today. You must know whether you can utilize the existing creative energy efficiently or whether you need to take action to increase creativity. Be persistent in pushing the team to know its level of creativity.

BALANCING REFLECTION AND INQUIRY: MANAGING THE DEBRIEFING EFFECTIVELY

A balance of *reflection* (thinking without actions) and *inquiry* (asking hard questions with the purpose of change) is very important to an effective debriefing.

In the work world, we must always gather as much information as possible, make our best assessment, and attempt to implement change through some form of action. The art in debriefing is knowing when to passively reflect (and let the group just stay where they are) and when to assertively inquire and move ahead with change (pushing them outside of their comfort zones).

In your debriefing, you will have to find the subtle balance between knowing when to push and when to back off in your attempt to help your client achieve maximum learning.

Kenny Rogers, in the famous song "The Gambler," sang: "You got to know when to hold 'em, know when to fold 'em, know when to walk away and know when to run." In the game of poker, players must pay attention to the reality of the game as any given moment and also to the reality that is imposed by the constant change induced by new cards being put on the table.

Managing a good debriefing is a very similar process.

Game Play

chapter four

Game Play Guidelines

In this chapter, we will help you understand how to facilitate the game by giving you supportive information, including:

1. A Participant's Guide

2. Trainer's Instructions

3. A Learn-o-grams™ Score Sheet

4. Master Answer Sheets

Let's start with the participant's guide. Give a copy of the following page to each participant before starting game play (see Participant's Guide on the CD-ROM). Read the instructions aloud and answer any questions participants may have. Then hand out the appropriate Learn-o-grams™ and score sheets for each team. Consult the Trainer's Instructions for details.

PARTICIPANT'S GUIDE

Objectives
To get the most points by guessing as many picture words correctly as possible within the time limit

Winner
The team with the most points at the end of three rounds

INSTRUCTIONS

1. *Form teams.* Divide into teams of equal size (in groups of between three and ten) and seat yourselves at tables with your teams. (Make sure that you can all see the screen.)

2. *Scoring.* Make sure that you have one score sheet for your team and that you select a scorekeeper. Your scorekeeper should write all answers that your team guesses on the score sheet, whether the answer is correct or just a guess. If the team cannot figure out an answer, the scorekeeper should just put an X in the space. (It is important to write down all answers for learning purposes.) The scorekeeper should tally your team's score at the end of each round.

3. *Categories.* Before proceeding, make sure that you understand the categories, which are as follows:
   - People (well-known celebrities, politicians, and so forth)
   - Places (cities, states, or countries)
   - Entertainment (the names of movies or TV shows)
   - Clichés (well-known sayings)

4. *Communication.* During game play, there should be no talking outside of your team. Whisper quietly to one another while trying to brainstorm and guess the answers at your table so that players at other tables cannot overhear you. At no time should you shout out an answer to another team, unless the facilitator requests that you do so. If you want to guess at an answer, talk through your ideas with other members of your team to increase your chances of getting the correct answer, and thus a higher score.

5. *Time limits.* The facilitator will set a time limit for figuring out each picture word. Do not begin work until told to do so and do not continue after the time is up.

 Learn-o-grams™

6. *Hints for guessing.* The picture words can usually be read from left to right and top to bottom, just like regular written pages. The following rules also apply to all cards:

- *A, an, the, and,* and *of* are usually omitted.

- Spaces between pictures always indicate separate words or names

- A plus sign (+) between two symbols means they are part of one word

- When guessing, consider the following options: sounds like, reverse order, expand or shrink a word or phrase, small words may be missing

● ●

TRAINER'S INSTRUCTIONS

Equipment Requirements
You will need a CD player, laptop computer with a projector, or any computer that connects with a large monitor or LCD projector. All images on the CD-ROM are in color.

Objective
To get the most points by guessing as many picture words correctly as possible within the time limit

Winner
The team with the most points at the end of any predetermined number of rounds wins (recommended rounds: three)

Table Arrangement
Round tables with up to ten players at each

Number of Players
(Ideally) Twenty-four to one hundred players in five to ten teams of four to six at tables

Minimum Number
Two teams with two players each

Note This game is designed for multiple players and multiple teams and is not suggested for one-on-one play.

Maximum Number
No maximum size limit, as long as everyone can see the screen; between 150 and 200 participants in fifteen to twenty teams of ten works well

Materials

- One CD, which contains ninety-six color pictures (twenty-four People, twenty-four Places, twenty-four Entertainment, and twenty-four Clichés)

- One copy of the Trainer's Instructions

- One copy of the Participant's Guide for each player

- One blank Score Sheet for each team

- One master set of answers in all categories for yourself

- The appropriate hard copies of the Learn-o-grams™, if desired

- Tent cards for tables

This version for the Learn-o-grams™ game is designed for medium and larger audiences and can be used on multiple occasions, as it has hundreds of possible combinations.

● ●

PREPARATION AND SETUP

1. Make sure that tables are as far apart as possible to avoid people hearing answers from other teams and to avoid the possibility of copying.

2. Put a number tent on each table and confirm that all participants know their table numbers. This way you can call out table numbers during scoring and debriefing.

3. Seating arrangement. There is no required seating as it does not matter whether players who know each other sit together. You can divide the entire group into teams of equal sizes and have them sit at separate tables or you can assign seating.

Slide Selection
Determine an order for the slides so that there is a happy medium between fun and challenge. Remember, you want the game to be challenging, but you also want the players to start to get the hang of it and show greater mastery as the game progresses.

1. Select between seven and ten Learn-o-grams™ in any category, depending on your time constraints.

2. Select two to four categories of Learn-o-grams™, by category, depending on how much time you have available (three sets of ten seems to work best).

3. You can either use all one category or mix the categories.

4. You may set different time limits for each category, if desired.

• •

PROCESS

Participant's Guides   Give each participant a copy of the guide, read through the instructions, and answer all questions before you begin. Supervise their dividing into teams and moving to tables.

Score Sheets   Give out score sheets, one to a table. Teams can make their own if necessary. Each team can make three equal columns on a blank sheet of paper (one per round), label each column by name (people, places, entertainment, or clichés) and number rows 1 through 10 down the page.

1. Remind each group to select a scorekeeper and to write down all their guesses on their sheets of paper, whether they are correct or incorrect, as they will use them later to analyze how their minds threw them off-track and how valuable even incorrect answers can be in getting to the right answer.

2. Explain that they will score by using the honor system.

Categories and Degree of Difficulty   Be sure all participants understand the categories of picture words they will be trying to find. Whether you are using all of one type of picture word or mixing and matching categories, make sure that you read and repeat the name of the category. If participants seem stuck, say the category again while they are working. Whenever you start a new category, say the name of that category out loud and repeat it, as each category has a different degree of difficulty.

COLOR/CATEGORY	LEVEL OF DIFFICULTY
Blue = People	Easiest
Orange = Places	Moderate Difficulty
Purple = Entertainment	More Difficult
Green = Clichés	Most Difficult

1. Set up your slide arrangements based on degree of difficulty and the audience need. Always balance easy game play and challenge. Err on the side of making it a little easier to play and find the answer; otherwise the game will be less fun.

2. Base your decisions on audience reaction. Always start with easy slides and then do a rough assessment of the participants' reactions. Often you won't know their true abilities until you have shown a few pictures. The following is a method of showing picture words based on ability:

   • Always start with the People category, because most of the people listed are relatively famous, most participants will have at least heard their names mentioned.

   • If participants are having a really hard time deciphering a Learn-o-grams™ picture, just show them another group from the People category or try a set of Places picture words—or give one clue per picture.

   • If the group is really proficient and guesses all the first set with ease, move on to Places or Entertainment.

   • If and only if they are super-achievers and guessing every one with ease, ask whether they would like to try some very difficult puzzles. If they say yes, try out a few Clichés. Be prepared to stop if participants find the picture words too difficult. Always think ahead and have a contingency plan in place.

   • The goal is to have the players feel good about their performance and to feel that they have improved in their ability to identify and figure out the logic of the Learn-o-grams™.

Estimated Time
Up to 15 minutes per round, including giving answers and discussion, with 30 to 45 minutes for a game with three or more rounds where each team guesses several words.

You will want to set up the order of pictures so that they go at a pace that keeps the audience hopping.

Time Per Picture
20 to 45 seconds, but you may change the time limit as necessary, based on audience requirements. Take more time if necessary, but watch out that the game doesn't begin to drag on.

Note
You can usually tell when the time is right to move on to the next picture because certain groups start chattering and laughing aloud instead of concentrating. Sometimes participants will do what I call, the "I got the answer" dance. This involves dancing motions similar to those of a football player who just made a touchdown.

1. Designate a timekeeper.

2. Have the person use a watch with a secondhand or a stop watch to keep time.

Checking Answers
When every team has finished a set of picture words, click back through the pictures on the screen. Have participants say their answers out loud one table at a time and then give the correct answers as they write in their scores or, if time is short, just ask, "What is the answer to this picture word?" and then confirm it when a player or team says the right one.

Difficulties
People may have difficulty playing this game for a number of reasons.

1. Some people do not read the newspaper.

2. They may not go the movies or watch TV.

3. Some younger people may not know many clichés.

4. People from different generations may not recognize the people.

5. People from other countries may not know the culture, ways, customs, and idiomatic sayings common in the United States.

6. Those who speak English as a second language may have difficulty.

Learn-o-grams™ has been designed based on the current American culture and the English language. No other language versions are in print at this time. The game is not recommended for entire groups composed only of those with English as a second language.

If participants are likely to have language issues, try to discuss the issue openly at the beginning of the game, stressing the fact that this can be a very difficult game because it uses idiomatic phrases and American cultural standards.

Ask permission to rearrange participants whose first language is not English so that they are well-integrated into tables with players who are strong in the English language. I have done this on numerous occasions with great results.

Solving the Puzzles Instantly
Highly intelligent participants or those I call "visual geniuses" may solve every puzzle instantly. I have discovered that about one in fifty of the general population can do this. These people will guess every answer immediately without thinking because their minds are wired in such a way as to allow them to see the answers almost instantaneously.

You may want to talk to these visual wizards during one of the breaks between categories and ask them to "hold back" a little to give their teammates a chance to enjoy game play. Obviously, if no one else on their team can guess an answer, they should by all means pitch in, but sometimes they need to give a little space to those who are less gifted.

Giving Clues

When playing the game using the CD-ROM, because participants are working in teams, clues are not usually given. The reasoning is that it is better to help the players test their assumptions. However, depending on the type of the group, you may want to give one or two general hints such as the following to help them develop some momentum.

1. The goal is to focus on the actual pictures as they are placed in the frame and to carefully analyze any relevance or meaning that this placement has.

2. To the degree that you look at each object within the picture word and analyze it individually, you will have a better idea of what you are trying to guess.

3. Focus on the *actions* in the picture words. Ask yourself, what, where, when, why, and how in regard to the actions taking place.

4. Ask yourself the three questions that follow about any Learn-o-grams™ puzzle:

- *Actions:* What actions are being applied to the items in the picture or being exerted by each part of the picture?

- *Placement:* How are the items placed in the picture? Is there any special meaning or significance to their locations?

- *Positional Power:* Does the item itself seem to have any special positional power or impact on other parts of the picture?

5. Always talk through your solutions out loud within your team to increase your score. By talking through the solutions, you may inadvertently give an answer that, although not correct, may jar or open the mind of another player.

Advancing the CD-ROM

It is important to advance the CD at just the right time, so if you are having someone else run the equipment, work out a system so that he or she understands when to project the next slide (if you are not using a remote control and doing it yourself). In this way, you can move ahead more quickly if everyone has finished or take more time if participants are having trouble with a slide.

LEARN-O-GRAMS
SCORESHEET™

Team Name (or number) _____

ROUND 1	ROUND 2	ROUND 3
Category	Category	Category
1.	1.	1.
2.	2.	2.
3.	3.	3.
4.	4.	4.
5.	5.	5.
6.	6.	6.
7.	7.	7.
8.	8.	8.
9.	9.	9.
10.	10.	10.
Subtotal	**Subtotal**	**Subtotal**
		Grand Total

Learn-o-grams™. Copyright © 2007 by John Wiley & Sons, Inc. Reproduced by permission of Pfeiffer, an Imprint of Wiley. www.pfeiffer.com

1. Art Linkletter
2. Barry Manilow
3. Beethoven
4. Bruce Springsteen
5. Cameron Diaz
6. David Letterman
7. Dr. Seuss
8. Eminem
9. Fidel Castro
10. Frankenstein
11. George W. Bush
12. Grandma Moses
13. Jack Nicholson
14. Jimmy Durante
15. Jim Nabors
16. Michelangelo
17. Paris Hilton
18. Penny Marshall
19. Ray Romano
20. Ronald Reagan
21. Ross Perot
22. Tom Cruise
23. Ty Cobb
24. Willie Nelson

1. Arkansas
2. Babylon
3. Baghdad
4. Belfast
5. Bucharest
6. Colorado
7. Concord
8. Dover
9. France
10. Iraq
11. Jefferson City
12. Little Rock

13. Milwaukee
14. Missouri
15. North Dakota
16. Rhode Island
17. Sacramento
18. Salt Lake City
19. Seattle
20. Singapore
21. Spokane
22. Trenton
23. Ukraine
24. Vienna

LEARN-O-GRAMS™ MASTER ANSWER SHEET—ENTERTAINMENT

1. 9 to 5
2. 101 Dalmatians
3. Addams Family
4. (The) Apprentice
5. (The) Brady Bunch
6. Cone Heads
7. Extreme Makeover
8. General Hospital
9. I Love Lucy
10. Little House on the Prairie
11. Nightline
12. Pelican Brief
13. Pet Cemetery
14. Peter Pan
15. Popeye
16. Real World
17. Sixth Sense
18. South Park
19. Spiderman
20. SpongeBob SquarePants
21. Star Trek
22. Survivor
23. Titanic
24. Wheel of Fortune

1. Ace in the hole
2. Back to square one
3. Breaking the ice
4. The buck stops here
5. A burning question
6. Called on the carpet
7. Compare apples to oranges
8. Cut a long story short
9. Dog eat dog
10. Don't beat around the bush
11. A drop in the bucket
12. Go for broke

13. Half-baked idea
14. I have a bone to pick
15. Lock, stock, and barrel
16. Loose cannon
17. No spring chicken
18. Not under any circumstances
19. On a rampage
20. One foot in the grave
21. Pass the buck
22. Rat race
23. Read between the lines
24. Sign of the times

The Learn-o-grams™

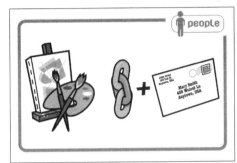

Picture Words: People

On the next page is an alphabetical listing of twenty-four famous, well-known People that corresponds to the full-page picture words that appear on the right-hand pages in this chapter.

Overall Level of Difficulty for This Category: Easy

"People" is one of the easiest categories because the people on the list are usually are well-known all over the world. Always start out with this category.

EACH LEFT-HAND PAGE CONTAINS

1. A description of the Learn-o-gram™ sketch

2. An explanation of the logic for each segment of the picture, to make it easier to explain the answers

3. A comment on common misconceptions that occur when typical participants try to solve the Learn-o-grams™

LEARN-O-GRAMS™ MASTER ANSWER SHEET—PEOPLE

1. Art Linkletter
2. Barry Manilow
3. Beethoven
4. Bruce Springsteen
5. Cameron Diaz
6. David Letterman
7. Dr. Seuss
8. Eminem
9. Fidel Castro
10. Frankenstein
11. George W. Bush
12. Grandma Moses
13. Jack Nicholson
14. Jimmy Durante
15. Jim Nabors
16. Michelangelo
17. Paris Hilton
18. Penny Marshall
19. Ray Romano
20. Ronald Reagan
21. Ross Perot
22. Tom Cruise
23. Ty Cobb
24. Willie Nelson

Learn-o-grams™. Copyright © 2007 by John Wiley & Sons, Inc. Reproduced by permission of Pfeiffer, an Imprint of Wiley. www.pfeiffer.com

Category	People
1	Art Linkletter
Rating	Easy

Description Art Linkletter had a famous TV show in the fifties and sixties and was known for his funny interviews with children

THE LOGIC

First Picture	An artist's pallet with a paintbrush
Second Picture	The links in a chain + (connected to)
Third Picture	A simple postal letter
Put it all together	art link + letter or Art Linkletter

COMMON MISPERCEPTIONS

1. People associate a paintbrush and wooden shape with the word "pallet."

2. Frequently, people mistake a link for a "chain."

3. The letter is often referred to as "mail."

I have had people shout, "pallet chain mail" to which I state, "Try again."

Category	People
2	Barry Manilow
Rating	Intermediate

Description Barry Manilow is a famous singer and performer of recent fame

THE LOGIC

First Picture | A fruit, but only the second half of the word, strawberry, is necessary—or just a berry

Second Picture | Two-part answer: (1) The mantle in the fireplace is actually the sill where you put items and (2) the location of the mantle, relatively low in comparison with the person in the picture

Put it all together | berry mantle + low or Barry Manilow

COMMON MISCONCEPTIONS

1. Frequently, people focus on the first part of the word, "straw."

2. Participants get stuck on the big picture, repeating the terms "fireplace" or "hearth" over and over again, instead of seeing a fireplace mantle.

3. Few people look at the location of the mantle in comparison to the height of the man.

Category	People
3	Beethoven
Rating	Easy to Intermediate

Description Beethoven was a prolific 17th century writers of classical music.

THE LOGIC

First Picture	A bee
Second Picture	A big toe
Third Picture	A van
Putting it all together	bee + toe + van or Beethoven

COMMON MISCONCEPTIONS

1. No problem with the bee.

2. No problem with the toe.

3. The van is harder to get because players call it a "truck" or a "car" or a "vehicle" instead of a van.

Note This is one picture word where many players just say the words "bee toe van" over and over again very slowly and somehow they always take a while to get the answer.

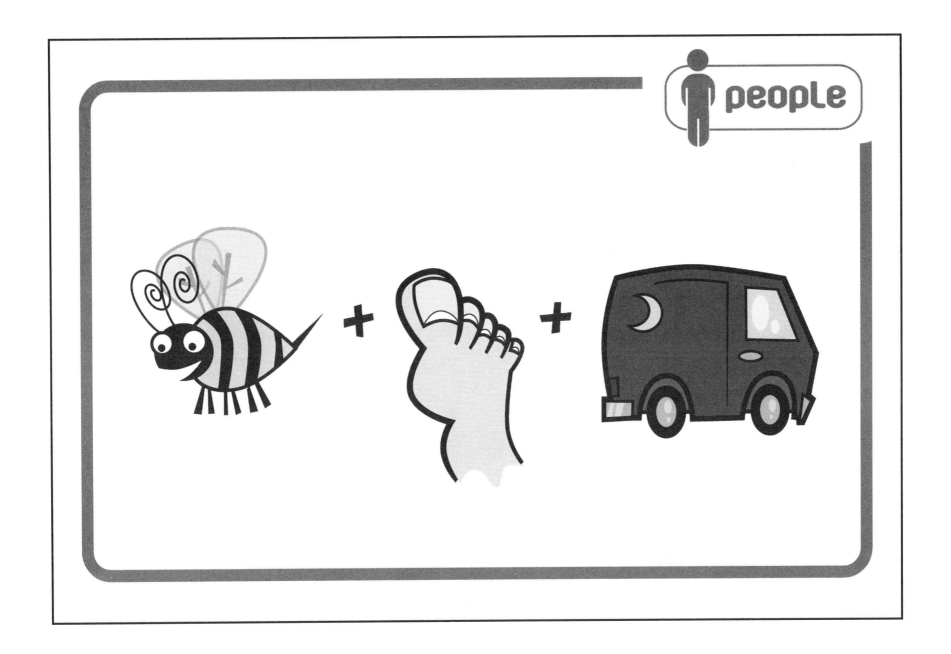

Category	People
4	Bruce Springsteen
Rating	Easy to Intermediate

Description Bruce Springsteen is a popular current singer and song-writer

THE LOGIC

First Picture	Mugs of beer or "brews"
Second Picture	(1) Three springs, (2) A cup of tea, (3) The letter N
Put it all together	brews springs + tea + n or Bruce Springsteen

COMMON MISCONCEPTIONS

1. Everyone thinks these are beer, cut-and-dried, and this is very ingrained in people's minds, although some people call them alcoholic beverages or cocktails.

2. Many people use the word "spring" instead of "springs" and this throws them off-track.

3. Most people put the second part of the word together first and then solve it backwards.

Learn-o-grams™

Category	People
5	Cameron Diaz
Rating	Intermediate
Description	Cameron Diaz is currently a famous Hollywood actress

THE LOGIC

Picture One	This is a single picture complex clue: (1) A camera, (2) The camera is "on" something, (3) A donkey or an "ass," (4) A descriptive letter "d"
Put it all together	camera + on "d" + ass or Cameron Diaz, just as it sounds

COMMON MISCONCEPTIONS

1. Players see the camera, but make no connection to its location "on top of" the donkey as significant.

2. Players see the donkey and call it a mule or donkey, afraid to call it an ass.

3. Players see the letter "d," but do not tie it in as a description connected with any of the other clue words.

Most participants just sit and look dumbfounded at this one for a while. You may want to give a little more time and also give the instruction (if they are having a hard time) to make sure that players look carefully at each segment of the single picture for clues.

Category	People
6	David Letterman
Rating	Intermediate to Difficult
Description	Dave Letterman is a famous late-night TV host

THE LOGIC

Picture One — (1) The calendar shows one "day" of the month and (2) The letter "v" combines with the word "day" to make "day-v" or "Dave"

Picture Two — (1) A simple postal letter, (2) Combines with a picture of a man

Put it all together — day + v letter + man or Dave Letterman

COMMON MISCONCEPTIONS

1. Very few people can isolate the word "day" from a calendar. Most think of the word "date," "page," "month," "15th," but few participants associate the simple word "day" with this clue. They also have trouble connecting it to the "v."

2. "Letter" and "man" are straightforward and simple.

Learn-o-grams™. Copyright © 2007 by John Wiley & Sons, Inc. Reproduced by permission of Pfeiffer, an Imprint of Wiley. www.pfeiffer.com

Category	People
7	Dr. Seuss
Rating	Easy

Description Dr. Seuss is a famous children's book writer known for his funny rhymes and books like *The Cat in the Hat*

THE LOGIC

Picture One	A physician or doctor in a lab coat with stethoscope and travel bag
Picture Two	The word "zoo" written four times to denote a group of "zoos," obviously a sound-alike
Put it all together	doctor and zoos or Dr. Seuss

COMMON MISCONCEPTIONS

1. The first word is simply "doctor."

2. In the second word, "zoo," many participants just look at and keep saying the word "zoo, zoo, zoo" and never say the plural, "zoos."

Category   People

8   Eminem

Rating   Easy to Intermediate

Description   Eminem is a prominent well-known rap star known for his unique rhythms and controversial lyrics

THE LOGIC

Picture One   A complex picture: (1) A giant three-dimensional "M," (2) A small m within the giant M

Put it all together The small m is within the giant three-dimensional M or it is an M in m, thus Eminem

COMMON MISCONCEPTIONS

1. For anyone over a certain age who does not know Eminem, this puzzle does not make any sense conceptually.

2. Some people just sit there saying M, M, M, over and over, with minimal connection. However, most young people figure out the puzzle clues pretty quickly because they are familiar with the name.

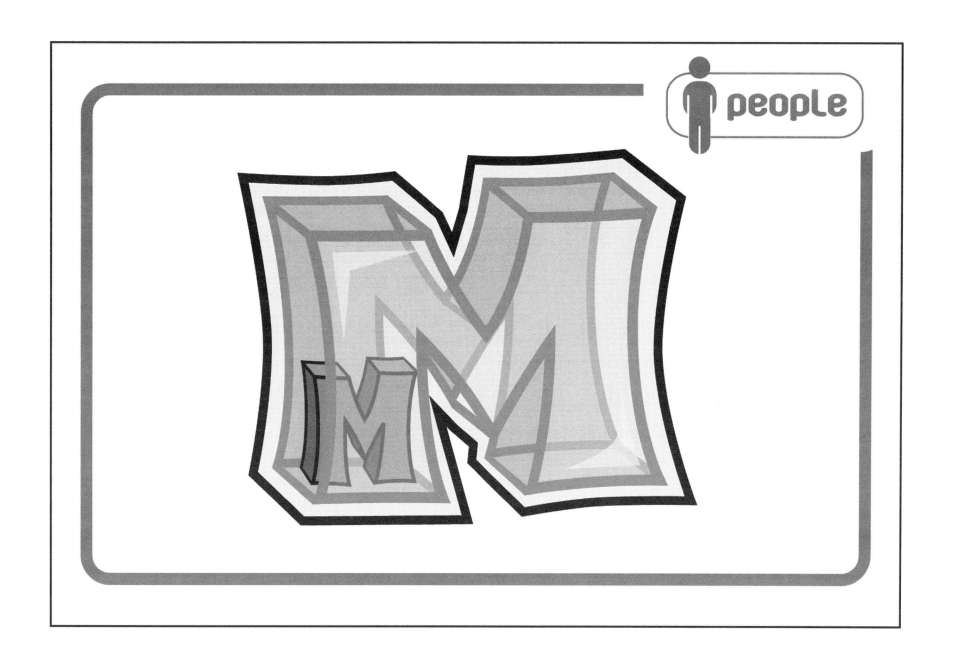

Category	People
9	Fidel Castro
Rating	Easy to Intermediate

Description Fidel Castro is the dictatorial self-proclaimed leader of Cuba and has been in charge for many, many years

THE LOGIC

Picture One	A fiddle, which sounds like Fidel
Picture Two	A cast on an arm
Picture Three	A person rowing a boat
Put it all together	fiddle + cast + row or Fidel Castro

COMMON MISCONCEPTIONS

1. Participants often think the first picture is a violin and will say "violin" several times before they realize that it is a fiddle. Even if they realize that it is a fiddle, they humorously sit there and say "fiddle cast row" over and over again.

2. The "cast" is obvious, but the person rowing the boat is harder, as players say "row boat" or "ores" or "boat."

Category	People
10	Frankenstein
Rating	Intermediate to Difficult

Description Frankenstein is a mythical movie creature, based on the book by Mary Shelley, supposedly made up of body parts from different people and brought to life by a mad scientist, only to wreak destruction on the town where he lived

THE LOGIC

Picture One	A complex single picture: (1) A "frank" or "frankfurter" is the German name for a hotdog, (2) A "stein," the German name for a mug
Putting it all together	A "frank" sitting inside of the "stein," or "frank in stein" or Frankenstein"

COMMON MISCONCEPTIONS

1. There is a hot dog sitting vertically. Some people call it by the alternative name, "weiner." No one ever thinks of the alternative name that it goes by in the ball park, which is a "frankfurter." The original German name also has a shortened version, simply called a "frank."

2. This is a glass container called by its German name, "stein." Many people call it a "mug," "cup," or "glass," but few think of "stein."

3. Even when people guess both words individually, they hysterically just keep repeating "frank in stein" over and over again until the inner light goes on.

Learn-o-grams™

Category	People
11	George W. Bush
Rating	Very Difficult

Description George W. Bush is, at the time of this writing, the President of the United States

THE LOGIC

Picture One	A gorge or large opening between two rocky, precipitous ledges
Picture Two	Two "U's" next to each other or a "double u"
Picture Three	A bush
Put it all together	gorge + UU + Bush or George W. Bush

COMMON MISCONCEPTIONS

1. The concept of a gorge is very difficult for most people and outside of their vocabulary. They call it a "cliff," "split rocks," "hole in the mountain," and "open rocks," but never a gorge.

2. Many people just keep saying, "U U" over and over again and never get the concept of a "double u," which creates the exact sound of the letter "W."

3. Participants call the "bush" a "shrub" or a "tree," but often miss the simple word "bush."

Learn-o-grams™. Copyright © 2007 by John Wiley & Sons, Inc. Reproduced by permission of Pfeiffer, an Imprint of Wiley. www.pfeiffer.com

THE LOGIC

Picture One — A complex picture: (1) An older woman, who could be a grandmother or "grandma," (2) A lawnmower mowing the grass, she "mows" the grass, (3) The shape of the cut area of the lawn is an S

Put it all together — A "grandma" who "mows" an "S" in the lawn or grandma mows + s or Grandma Moses.

COMMON MISCONCEPTIONS

1. Everyone sees that this is an older woman and will say, "woman" or "old woman" or "lady" or "old lady." Few people catch on and think about the fact that she could be a grandmother or "grandma," as she might affectionately be known.

2. Most people see and say "lawnmower," but do not think of the action of mowing or the present tense, "mow."

3. Most people see the shape of the S, but few put together the entire concept easily.

4. However, once they get "mows" + "s," they figure out the rest pretty quickly.

Category	People
13	Jack Nicholson
Rating	Easy

Description Jack Nicholson is a famous actor who has appeared in dozens of movies and is known for his "off-the-wall" parts

THE LOGIC

Picture One	A simple "jack" from a children's game
Picture Two	A five-cent piece or a "nickel"
Picture Three	The sun
Put it all together	jack + nickel + sun or Jack Nicholson

COMMON MISCONCEPTIONS

1. This is a relatively easy puzzle.

2. He is an older actor, and thus many younger participants have not heard of him.

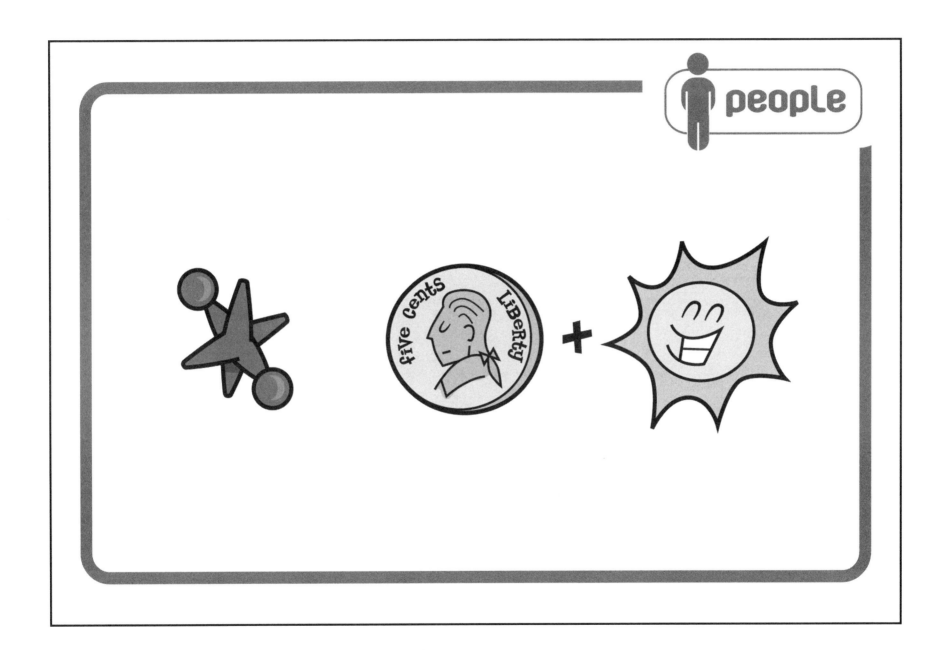

Learn-o-grams™. Copyright © 2007 by John Wiley & Sons, Inc. Reproduced by permission of Pfeiffer, an Imprint of Wiley. www.pfeiffer.com

Category	People
14	Jimmy Durante
Rating	Easy

Description Jimmy Durante was a famous entertainer and singer from the early 20th century who was known for making fun of his own big nose, which he called a "schnazolla"

THE LOGIC

Picture One	An ice cream cone with colored sugar sprinkles or "jimmies" on it
Picture Two	A door
Picture Three	An ant
Picture Four	The letter E
Put it all together	jimmie + door + ant + e or Jimmy Durante

COMMON MISCONCEPTIONS

1. Most people know that the colored sugar sprinkles that you put on an ice cream cone are called "jimmies," but there are some geographical areas in which they are called "sprinkles."

2. People put the words "door ant e" together right away, but many younger people have never heard of this old-time entertainer.

Category	People
15	Jim Nabors
Rating	Difficult

Description Jim Nabors was one of the stars of a comedy show from the sixties called "The Andy Griffith Show" and later was in many movies and was also a great singer

THE LOGIC

Picture One

A single complex picture: (1) The name "Jim" is on every mail box and thus a common word to the puzzle, (2) All the houses are in the same close vicinity and thus they are all "neighbors"

Put it all together

Jim and neighbors or Jim Nabors

COMMON MISCONCEPTIONS

1. This is a very difficult puzzle to solve because both clues are a little vague and diffuse in their connection.

2. "Jim" is the common name on all three mailboxes; however, I have had people guess the words "mail" or "mailbox" or say, "You've got mail."

3. The close proximity of the houses is the key to figuring out that the people who live there are neighbors. Because the houses are in the background, it is a little harder to grasp.

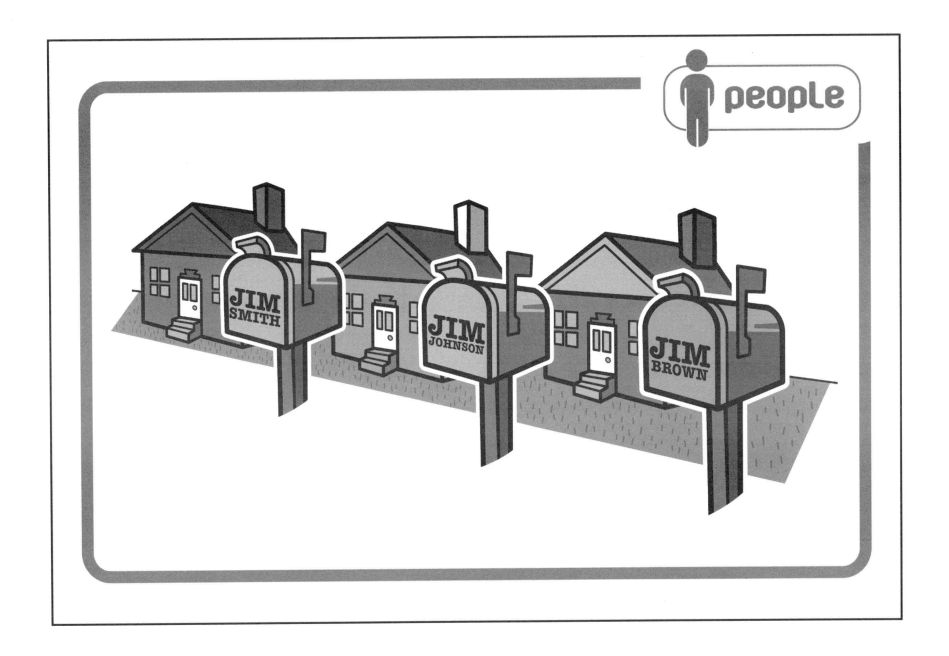

Category	People
16	Michelangelo
Rating	Easy to Intermediate

Description Michelangelo was a world-renowned artist who spent many years painting the ceiling of the Sistine Chapel in Rome during the Rennaisance

THE LOGIC

Picture One	A microphone or "mike" for short
Picture Two	A creature in hell
Picture Three	An angel
Picture Four	An overdue bill on which someone "owes" money
Put it all together	mike + hell + angel + owe or Michelangelo

COMMON MISCONCEPTIONS

1. Participants get most of this puzzle right away because it is conveniently broken down into simple phonetic segments.

2. Players do have a little problem with the concept of the second picture word, often calling it the "devil" and then finally realizing it is "hell."

3. The last picture of an overdue bill is also difficult for players because they say "bill" or "payment" instead of "owe."

Category	People
17	Paris Hilton
Rating	Easy

Description Paris Hilton is a famous young celebrity and singer who starred in a tv show titled "The Simple Life"

THE LOGIC

Picture One	A pear with an S in the middle
Picture Two	A hill
Picture Three	A 2,000-pound weight, which equals one ton
Put it all together	pear + S, a hill + ton or Paris Hilton

COMMON MISCONCEPTIONS

1. Sometimes players can't figure out that the S in the picture of the pear is part of the answer or they say "S pear" or "spear" instead of "pear S."

2. Some participants don't know that 2,000 pounds equals a ton.

Category	People
18	Penny Marshall
Rating	Intermediate

Description Penny Marshall was the costar of a popular TV show, "Laverne and Shirley," for many years, and later went on to become a talented director and producer in Hollywood

THE LOGIC

Picture One	A penny
Picture Two	A lawman or marshal from the old wild
Put it all together	Penny Marshall

COMMON MISCONCEPTIONS

1. The "penny" is straightforward and obvious.

2. The "marshal" is harder to guess. Participants call this a "sheriff" or "policeman" or a "lawman" or a "cop," but "marshal" is very elusive and not commonly used.

people

Learn-o-grams™. Copyright © 2007 by John Wiley & Sons, Inc. Reproduced by permission of Pfeiffer, an Imprint of Wiley. www.pfeiffer.com

Category	People
19	Ray Romano
Rating	Easy

Description Ray Romano is a popular comic who starred in his own TV show called "Everybody Loves Raymond"

THE LOGIC

Picture One	A "sting*ray*" from the ocean
Picture Two	A "Roman" soldier in full uniform
Picture Three	The letter "O"
Put it all together	ray + Roman + O or Ray Romano

COMMON MISCONCEPTIONS

1. Players almost always get the stingray or just a "ray," which is one of its nicknames.

2. For some reason, participants have a hard time with the Roman soldier and will often get sidetracked with guesses like "soldier," "warrior," "spear," or "helmet."

Learn-o-grams™. Copyright © 2007 by John Wiley & Sons, Inc. Reproduced by permission of Pfeiffer, an Imprint of Wiley. www.pfeiffer.com

Category	People
20	Ronald Reagan
Rating	Difficult

Description Ronald Reagan was a two-term U.S. President who was a famous radio, TV, and movie actor for many years before being elected governor of California

THE LOGIC

Picture One	A complex single picture: (1) An old man and (2) The person is running
Picture Two	A space invader's futuristic or cartoon-like ray gun
Putting it all together	run + old and ray + gun or Ronald Reagan

COMMON MISCONCEPTIONS

1. The first picture is very difficult unless players figure out the second picture and then work backwards. An old man is running, and thus the concept of "running old" or "run old," which sounds like Ronald.

2. The ray gun is usually obvious.

Category	People
21	Ross Perot
Rating	Easy

Description A successful businessman who ran unsuccessfully for President of the United States in 1992

THE LOGIC

Picture One	A rose
Picture Two	A pear
Picture Three	A person rowing a boat
Putting it all together	rose + pear + row or Ross Perot

COMMON MISCONCEPTIONS

1. The rose is actually a sound-alike for Ross.

2. The pear is for the first part of his name.

3. Some people may focus on the boat and not the action of rowing.

4. The younger generation may not have heard of him.

Category	People
22	Tom Cruise
Rating	Easy to Intermediate

Description Tom Cruise is a Hollywood actor who is known for his action roles (*Mission Impossible* series) and many other movies

THE LOGIC

Picture One	A "tom-tom" drum
Picture Two	A large ocean liner or a "cruise" ship
Putting it all together	Tom Cruise

COMMON MISCONCEPTIONS

1. The tom-tom drum is always easy.

2. The cruise ship is pretty easy too, but sometimes players call it a "boat" or "ocean liner."

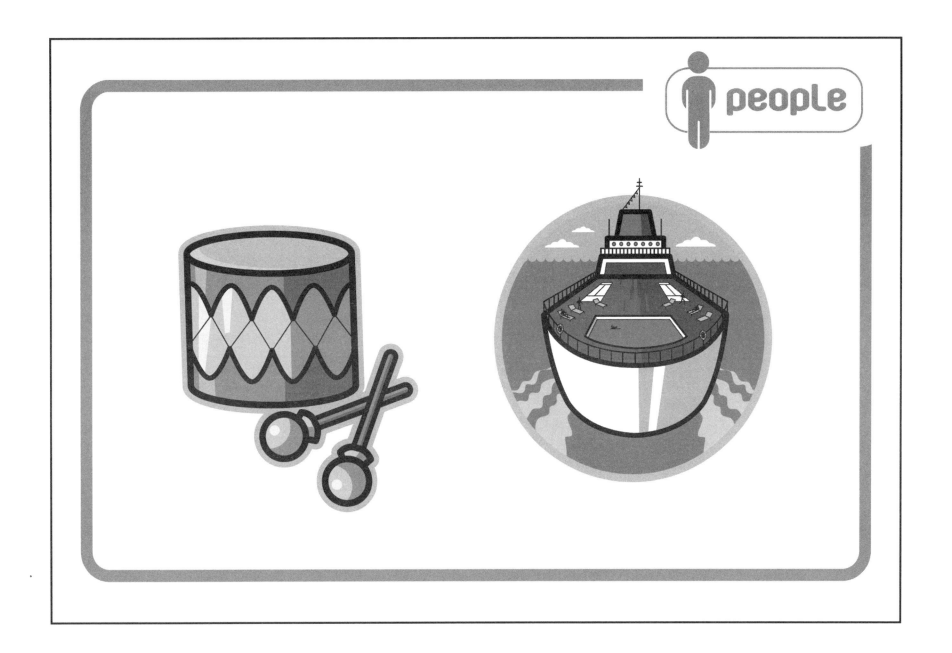

Category	People
23	Ty Cobb
Rating	Intermediate

Description Ty Cobb was a world-renowned baseball player in the 1920s and 1930s.

THE LOGIC

Picture One	A complex single picture: (1) A stalk of corn, which is actually corn on the "cob" and (2) The corn is wearing a tie
Putting it all together	tie on corn on the cob or Ty Cobb

COMMON MISCONCEPTIONS

1. This is a hard one for people to pull apart because it is a little abstract. The tie is fine by itself, and they guess this immediately.

2. The "cob" of corn is less obvious and takes a little trial-and-error guessing.

3. Watching people combining the two in this cartoon-like puzzle is very humorous.

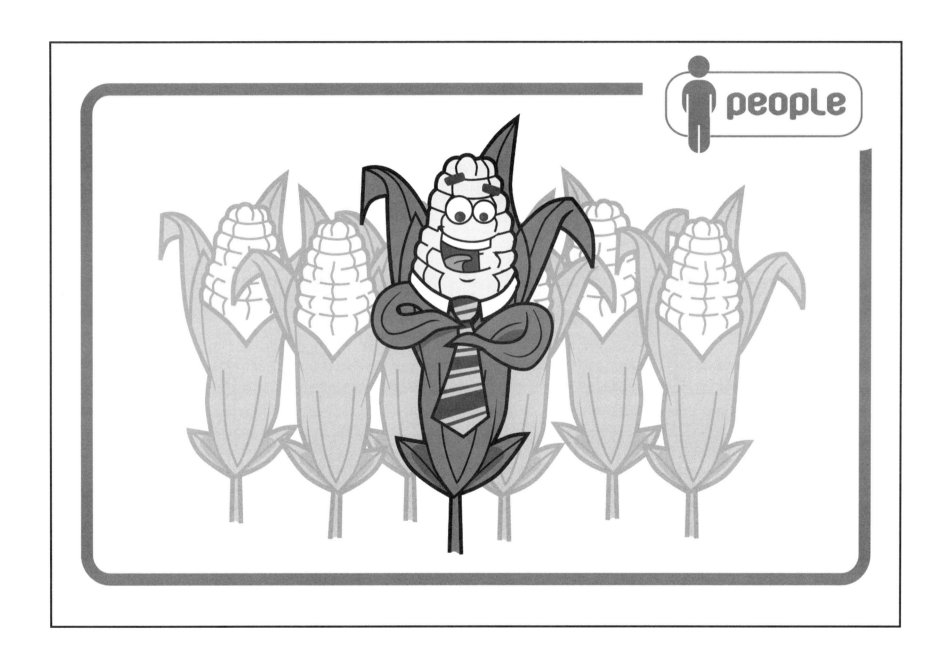

Category	People
24	Willie Nelson
Rating	Easy

Description Willie Nelson is a long-time country-western singer who has been in many TV shows and movies and has written over two thousand songs

THE LOGIC

Picture One	Last "will" and testament
Picture Two	The letter "e"
Picture Three	A "nail"
Picture Four	The "sun"
Put it all together	will + e and nail + sun or Willie Nelson

COMMON MISCONCEPTIONS

1. This is a very straightforward, simple puzzle.

Picture Words: Places

On the next page is an alphabetical list of twenty-four Places (cities, states, or countries) that corresponds to the full-page picture words on the right-hand pages in this chapter.

Overall Level of Difficulty for This Category: Easy to Intermediate

"Places" is a little more difficult category because geography is often studied minimally in modern schools. Generational differences abound, especially among younger people, who seem to have less grasp of general geography.

One last point: a good portion of the geography for this version is North-American-based. Future versions will be more global in nature so as to offer greater diversity.

EACH LEFT-HAND PAGE CONTAINS

1. A description of the Learn-o-gram™ sketch

2. An explanation of the logic for each segment of the picture, to make it easier to explain the answers

3. A comment on common misconceptions that occur when typical participants try to solve the Learn-o-grams™

LEARN-O-GRAMS™ MASTER ANSWER SHEET—PLACES

1. Arkansas
2. Babylon
3. Baghdad
4. Belfast
5. Bucharest
6. Colorado
7. Concord
8. Dover
9. France
10. Iraq
11. Jefferson City
12. Little Rock
13. Milwaukee
14. Missouri
15. North Dakota
16. Rhode Island
17. Sacramento
18. Salt Lake City
19. Seattle
20. Singapore
21. Spokane
22. Trenton
23. Ukraine
24. Vienna

Category	Places
1	Arkansas
Rating	Easy
Description	Arkansas is a state in the Southern United States

THE LOGIC

First Picture	An "ark" or a large boat considered the transportation that Noah used to move the animals
Second Picture	A can
Third Picture	A saw
Put it all together	ark + can + saw or Arkansas

COMMON MISCONCEPTIONS

1. Once participants figure out that the boat is the ark, the rest is very easy. At first players say "boat" or "ship," but then they see the animals and the lone man standing in front of the boat, most players easily identify it as the ark.

2. "Can" and "saw" are immediately recognizable.

Learn-o-grams™. Copyright © 2007 by John Wiley & Sons, Inc. Reproduced by permission of Pfeiffer, an Imprint of Wiley. www.pfeiffer.com

Category	Places
2	Babylon
Rating	Easy

Description Babylon is the ancient name for Iraq, a country in the Middle East

THE LOGIC

First Picture   A baby

Second Picture   A lawn with green grass

Put it all together   A baby sitting on a lawn or "baby lawn" or Babylon

COMMON MISCONCEPTIONS

1. Although both words are easy to guess individually, participants have some degree of difficulty putting them together in a logical way and often say "baby lawn" or "lawn baby" several times before the connection is made.

Learn-o-grams™. Copyright © 2007 by John Wiley & Sons, Inc. Reproduced by permission of Pfeiffer, an Imprint of Wiley. www.pfeiffer.com

Category	Places
3	Baghdad
Rating	Easy to Intermediate
Description	Baghdad is a city in the Middle East and is the capital of Iraq

THE LOGIC

First Picture	A single complex picture: (1) A bag and (2) A sign that says "Happy Father's Day!"
Put it all together	A "bag" that belongs to "dad," or bag dad or Baghdad

COMMON MISCONCEPTIONS

1. Players have no trouble identifying both parts of the puzzle, but take a while to put together the pieces.

2. Many participants sit there and say "bag Father's Day" several times, or even say the actual words "Bag Dad" over and over before getting it.

Category	Places
4	Belfast
Rating	Easy to Intermediate
Description	A city in Northern Ireland

THE LOGIC

First Picture	A complex single picture: (1) A bell with arms and legs and (2) The bell is running fast
Put it all together	A bell running fast or Belfast

COMMON MISCONCEPTIONS

1. Although this is also a simple puzzle, players often say "a bell that is running" or "ring and run," but it is difficult to make the association with a bell that runs fast.

Note Remind them of the category and make sure you redefine it any time they get stuck.

Learn-o-grams™. Copyright © 2007 by John Wiley & Sons, Inc. Reproduced by permission of Pfeiffer, an Imprint of Wiley. www.pfeiffer.com

Category	Places
5	Bucharest
Rating	Easy to Intermediate
Description	A city and the capital of Romania

THE LOGIC

First Picture	A single complex picture: (1) A book with arms and legs and (2) The book is being arrested and put into the back of a squad car
Put it all together	A book being arrested, or "book arrest" or Bucharest

COMMON MISCONCEPTIONS

1. This gives the impression of a simple scene; however, participants say things like, "a bad book" or a "book about trouble" or "the police."

2. It often takes players a little while to get this.

Category	Places
6	Colorado
Rating	Very Easy

Description Colorado is a state in the Rocky Mountains of the United States

THE LOGIC

First Picture	A dog collar
Second Picture	A fishing rod
Third Picture	A mound of dough with a rolling pin
Put it all together	collar + rod + dough or Colorado

COMMON MISCONCEPTIONS

1. This is a very easy puzzle with no real complications.

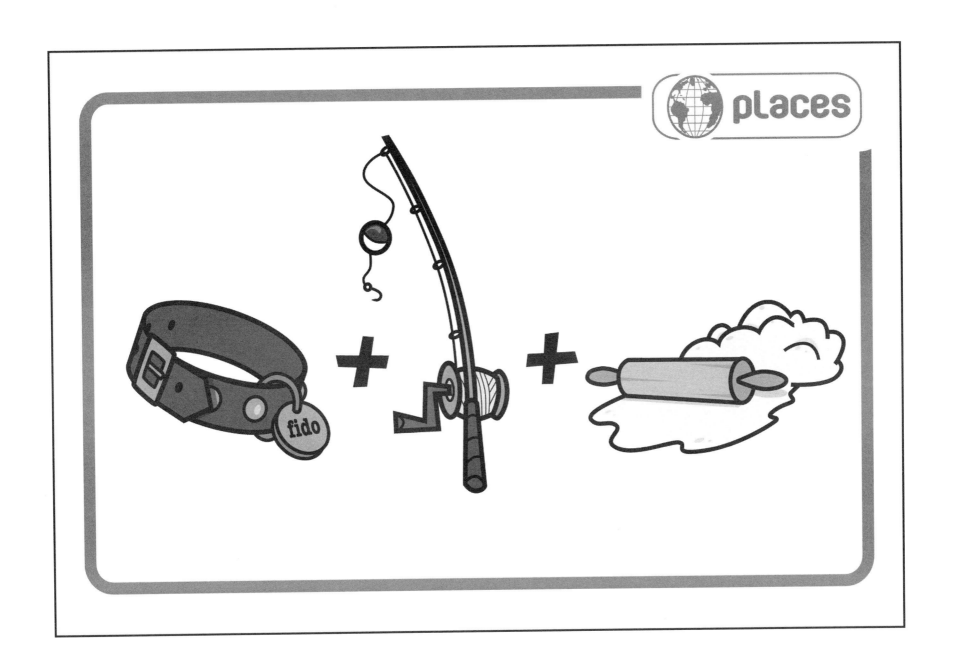

Learn-o-grams™. Copyright © 2007 by John Wiley & Sons, Inc. Reproduced by permission of Pfeiffer, an Imprint of Wiley. www.pfeiffer.com

Category	Places
7	Concord
Rating	Easy to Intermediate

Description Concord is the capital of New Hampshire, a state in the Northeastern United States

THE LOGIC

First Picture	A convict or "con" man
Second Picture	A telephone cord
Put it all together	con and cord or Concord

COMMON MISCONCEPTIONS

1. Guessing the first picture word is actually very difficult. Many players guess a "prisoner," an "inmate," a "criminal," or a "jail bird." Because the word "con" is not a commonly used name for a convict, this is a stumper.

2. The telephone cord is also a little difficult because people say "telephone," "headset," or "connection," and often don't think of "cord."

Learn-o-grams™. Copyright © 2007 by John Wiley & Sons, Inc. Reproduced by permission of Pfeiffer, an Imprint of Wiley. www.pfeiffer.com

Category	Places
8	Dover
Rating	Easy

Description Dover is the capital of Delaware, a very small Mid-Atlantic state

THE LOGIC

First Picture	A dove
Second Picture	The letter R
Put it all together	dove and R or Dover

COMMON MISCONCEPTIONS

1. Because of the short "o" sound (uh) in the word "dove," players have a bit of a hard time making the leap from dove to the long "oh" sound. However, once they say it a few times and realize that the category is Places, the job gets much easier.

Picture Words: Places

Category	Places
9	France
Rating	Easy to Intermediate

Description   France is a country in Western Europe bordering Belgium, Spain, and Italy.

THE LOGIC

First Picture	A fur stole or small fur piece
Second Picture	Two ants
Put it all together	fur + ants or France

COMMON MISCONCEPTIONS

1. The word "fur" is actually quite hard because people focus on the woman in the picture and say "woman" or "model" or "jewelry." Finally, when they see the fur they say "fox" or "coat" or "jacket." With a little effort, they figure out that it is a fur.

2. The problem with the ants is that very few people actually know what ants look like up close because they are so small. Players say "bugs" or "pests" or "beetles" or "cockroach."

Learn-o-grams™. Copyright © 2007 by John Wiley & Sons, Inc. Reproduced by permission of Pfeiffer, an Imprint of Wiley. www.pfeiffer.com

Category	Places
10	Iraq
Rating	Easy to Intermediate
Description	Iraq is a country in the Middle East

THE LOGIC

First Picture	A coat rack
Second Picture	A bunch of hanging "I's"
Put it all together	i's hanging on a coat rack or an "I rack" or Iraq

COMMON MISCONCEPTIONS

1. The coat rack is easy to guess.

2. Connecting the hanging I's to the name Iraq is rather complex abstract thinking. The hanging I's are on the rack and, just as if clothing were hanging there it would be called a clothes rack, so this is an "I rack" or a rack filled with I's. People say, "I's rack" or "ice rack" or "falling I's," but often miss the simple connection.

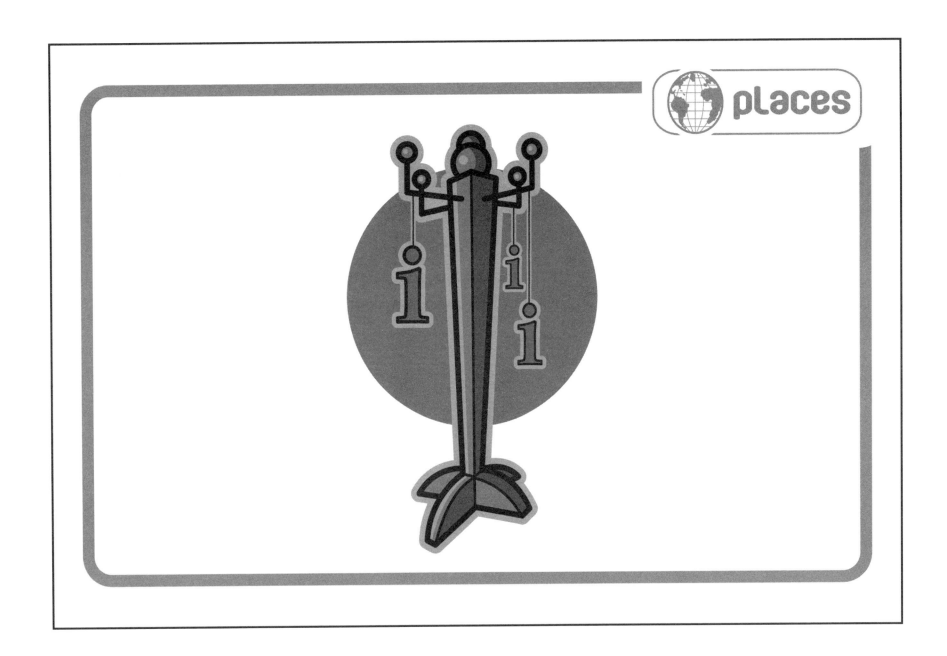

Category	Places
11	Jefferson City
Rating	Easy

Description Jefferson City is the capital of Missouri in the Midwestern United States

THE LOGIC

First Picture	A chef
Second Picture	A fur
Third Picture	The sun
Fourth Picture	A little lifelike "T" sitting in a chair
Put it all together	chef + fur + sun + sitting T or Jefferson City

COMMON MISCONCEPTIONS

1. Most of the symbols in this puzzle have been used before or are very easy to decipher.

2. However, people get stuck on the first picture. Few people guess that it is a "chef" right off the bat. People say this is a "butcher" or a "cook" or "kitchen help."

Category	Places
12	Little Rock
Rating	Easy

Description Little Rock is the capital of Arkansas, in the Southern United States

THE LOGIC

Picture One	A single complex picture that is a comparison of two rocks
Put it all together	There is a big rock next to a little rock with the arrow pointing at the little rock, so the answer is Little Rock

COMMON MISCONCEPTIONS

1. This puzzle is pretty straightforward and, although it takes a little thinking to get the answer, it is very intuitive.

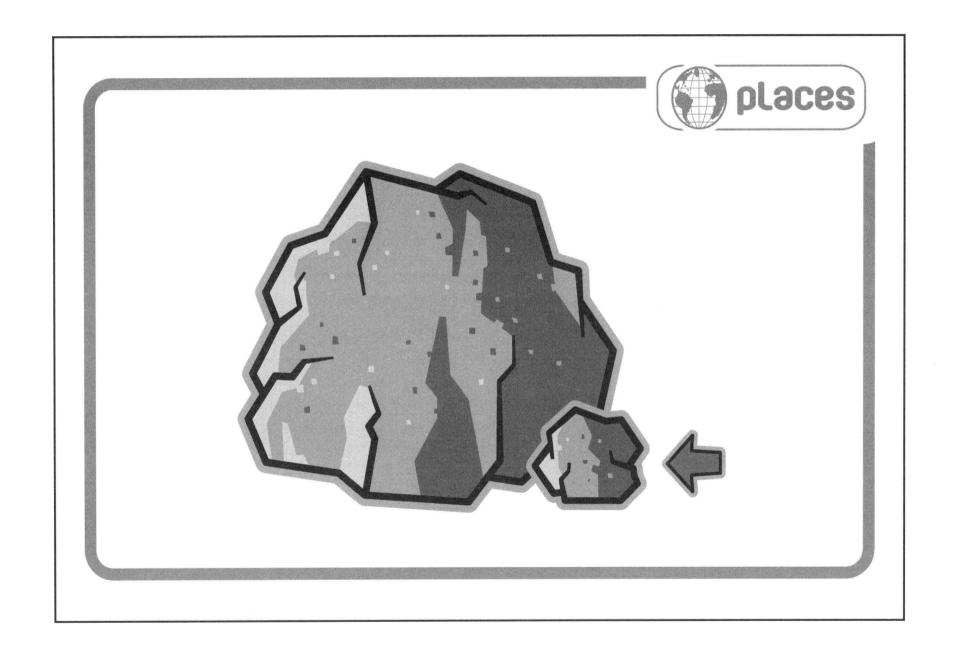

Learn-o-grams™. Copyright © 2007 by John Wiley & Sons, Inc. Reproduced by permission of Pfeiffer, an Imprint of Wiley. www.pfeiffer.com

Category	Places
13	Milwaukee
Rating	Easy

Description Milwaukee is a city in Wisconsin, located in the Midwestern United States

THE LOGIC

First Picture	An old-fashioned mill with a water wheel turning
Second Picture	A man walking
Third Picture	A key
Put it all together	mill + walk + key or Milwaukee

COMMON MISCONCEPTIONS

1. The only glitch in this picture word is figuring out what the building with the big wheel located right next to the water is. The older generation would more likely have seen one of these old-fashioned mills (for grinding grain or generating power) in their youth, and so it is easier for them to solve the puzzle.

2. However, some of the younger generation of players have said this is a "house by the water" or a "hydro-electric dam" or an "electric generating plant."

Learn-o-grams™. Copyright © 2007 by John Wiley & Sons, Inc. Reproduced by permission of Pfeiffer, an Imprint of Wiley. www.pfeiffer.com

Category	Places
14	Missouri
Rating	Easy to Intermediate
Description	Missouri is a state in the Midwestern United States

THE LOGIC

First Picture	An arrow "missing" its target
Second Picture	An oar
Third Picture	An eye
Put it all together	miss + oar + eye or Missouri

COMMON MISCONCEPTIONS

1. The most difficult part of this picture word is figuring out that the first picture is of an arrow missing the mark. Participants say "arrow" or "target" or "archery" until they start to think outside the box and realize that the arrow is missing the target to create the word "miss."

2. The word "oar" is simple, but the word "eye" is difficult because it is a sound-alike. The word eye is similar but different from the long "e" sound at the end of "Missouri."

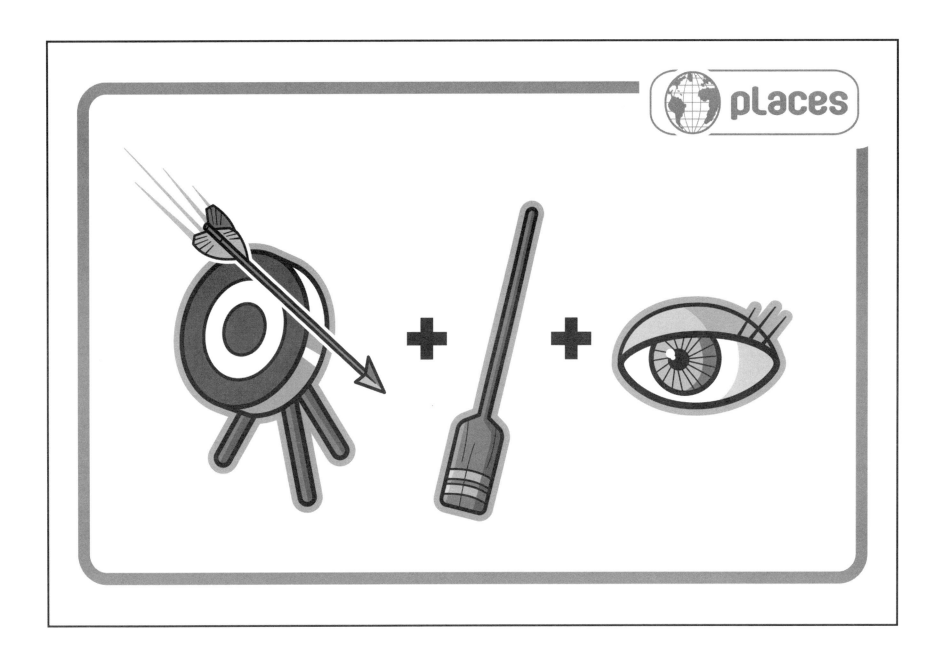

Learn-o-grams™. Copyright © 2007 by John Wiley & Sons, Inc. Reproduced by permission of Pfeiffer, an Imprint of Wiley. www.pfeiffer.com

<table>
<tr><td>Category</td><td>Places</td></tr>
<tr><td>15</td><td>North Dakota</td></tr>
<tr><td>Rating</td><td>Easy</td></tr>
<tr><td>Description</td><td>North Dakota is a state in the north-central United States</td></tr>
</table>

THE LOGIC

First Picture	An arrow that faces north
Second Picture	The letter "D" and the sound "de"
Third Picture	A coat
Fourth Picture	The letter "A" and the sound "ah"
Put it all together	north + D + coat + ah or North Dakota

COMMON MISCONCEPTIONS

1. There are no complex parts to this puzzle.

Category	Places
16	Rhode Island
Rating	Easy to Intermediate

Description Rhode Island is an extremely small state on the East Coast of the United States

THE LOGIC

First Picture	A single complex picture: (1) A very tiny "island" and (2) A "road" all the way across the island
Put it all together	A road across most of the island or road island or Rhode Island

COMMON MISCONCEPTIONS

1. The parts of this puzzle are rather easy. However, conceptually tying together the fact that there is a road and the fact that it runs clear across the island has stumped some players.

Learn-o-grams™. Copyright © 2007 by John Wiley & Sons, Inc. Reproduced by permission of Pfeiffer, an Imprint of Wiley. www.pfeiffer.com

THE LOGIC

First Picture	A large sack of flour
Second Picture	A man rowing a boat
Third Picture	Two men having a conversation
Fourth Picture	A toe
Put it all together	sack + row + men + toe or Sacramento

COMMON MISCONCEPTIONS

1. People often have a hard time figuring out what the sack of flour is. However, since the rest of the puzzle is so easy, they solve that part first and then have no problem sounding out the answer.

Learn-o-grams™

Learn-o-grams™. Copyright © 2007 by John Wiley & Sons, Inc. Reproduced by permission of Pfeiffer, an Imprint of Wiley. www.pfeiffer.com

Category	Places
18	Salt Lake City
Rating	Very Easy

Description Salt Lake City is the capital of Utah, in the intermountain area of the United States

THE LOGIC

First Picture	A salt shaker
Second Picture	A lake
Third Picture	A "T" sitting in a chair
Put it all together	salt and lake and a sitting T or Salt Lake City

COMMON MISCONCEPTIONS

1. This is a very easy puzzle because each part of it is straightforward and many of the picture words have been used before.

Category	Places
19	Seattle
Rating	Easy to Intermediate

Description   Seattle is a large city in Oregon, in the Northwestern United States

THE LOGIC

First Picture   A complex single picture: (1) The letter "C" over the letter "L" and (2) A plus sign to the left and an underscore beneath

Put it all together   "C," add "L," or Seattle

COMMON MISCONCEPTIONS

1. The difficult part of this puzzle is trying to differentiate the plus sign and what it means. Most players just say "C plus L" over and over again.

2. The obvious secret is that the plus sign means "add" in mathematics, which is a sound-alike for "at."

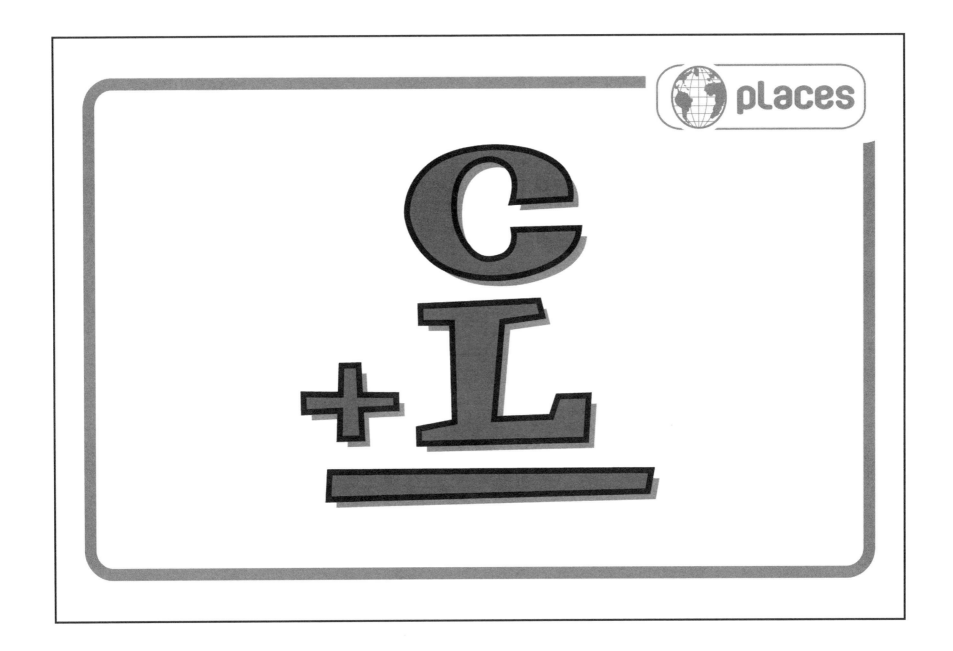

Picture Words: Places

Learn-o-grams™. Copyright © 2007 by John Wiley & Sons, Inc. Reproduced by permission of Pfeiffer, an Imprint of Wiley. www.pfeiffer.com

Category	Places
20	Singapore
Rating	Easy
Description	Singapore is a country in Asia

THE LOGIC

First Picture	A person singing in front of a microphone
Second Picture	A pitcher of water pouring into a glass
Third Picture	The letter "A" on the pitcher
Put it all together	Singing and pouring water where the pitcher has the letter A on it, so it is literally sing + a + pour or Singapore

COMMON MISCONCEPTIONS

1. No real difficulties or complexities except trying to fit the "a" in the proper place between "sing" and "pour."

Category	Places
21	Spokane
Rating	Intermediate to Difficult
Description	Spokane is a city in Washington State

THE LOGIC

First Picture	A single complex picture: (1) A wheel and (2) A set of spokes that are made of candy canes
Put it all together	spokes of a wheel made out of candy canes or "spoke" "cane" or Spokane

COMMON MISCONCEPTIONS

1. This is very difficult to guess because there are so many abstractions.

2. Players will focus on the wheel and on the candy canes. In fact, they can guess each of these components pretty quickly on an individual basis, but do not connect them.

3. Players will say the word "wheels" over and over again. The problem is that the focus has to be on the spokes that are made of candy canes, and this requires a great deal of group brainstorming.

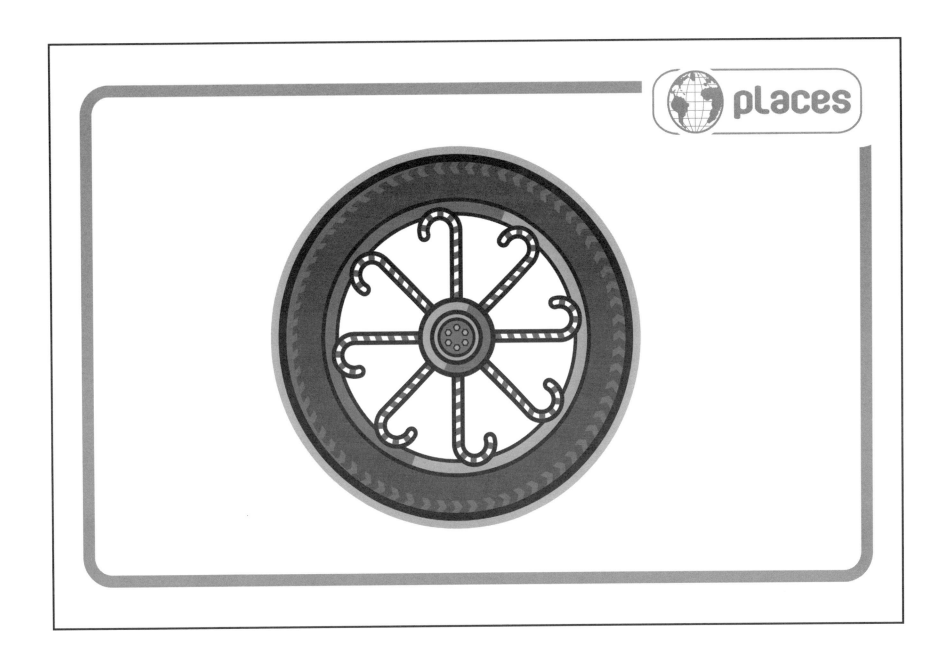

Category	Places
22	Trenton
Rating	Easy

Description Trenton is the capital of New Jersey, in the Eastern United States

THE LOGIC

First Picture	The locomotive of a train
Second Picture	A 2,000-pound weight
Put it all together	train + ton or Trenton, which is a sound-alike

COMMON MISCONCEPTIONS

1. A relatively easy puzzle with two simple words.

2. The trick is getting the sound-alike for "train" and knowing that 2,000 pounds is a ton.

Category	Places
23	Ukraine
Rating	Easy

Description Ukraine is in Eastern Europe, bordering the Black Sea, between Poland, Romania, and Moldova in the west and Russia to the east

THE LOGIC

First Picture	A large crane
Second Picture	The big letter "U" being lifted up
Put it all together	A crane picking up the letter U or a "U crane" or Ukraine

COMMON MISCONCEPTIONS

1. No complexities, very straightforward.

Picture Words: Places

Category	Places
24	Vienna
Rating	Easy to Intermediate

Description Vienna is the capital of Austria and is in Central Europe, north of Italy and Slovenia

THE LOGIC

First Picture	A single complex picture: (1) A large three-dimensional letter "A" and (2) A small letter "V" inside the lower-left section of the "A"
Put it all together	The V is inside the A or it is a "V in A" or Vienna

COMMON MISCONCEPTIONS

1. The only understanding necessary to solve this puzzle is to realize that the letter V is indeed inside the big hollow letter A.

Picture Words:
Entertainment

On the next page is an alphabetical list of twenty-four picture cards in the Entertainment category (TV shows or movies) that corresponds with the full-page picture words on the right-hand pages later in the chapter.

Overall Level of Difficulty of This Category: Easy to Intermediate

"Entertainment" is usually relatively easy because so many of the Hollywood productions are well-known all over the world. Of course, there is still a strong generational bias and a player's knowledge can also be dependent on the culture he or she is from.

EACH LEFT-HAND PAGE CONTAINS

1. A description of the Learn-o-gram™ sketch

2. An explanation of the logic for each segment of the picture, to make it easier to explain the answers

3. A comment on common misconceptions that occur when typical participants try to solve the Learn-o-grams™

LEARN-O-GRAMS™ MASTER ANSWER SHEET—ENTERTAINMENT

1. 9 to 5

2. 101 Dalmatians

3. (The) Addams Family

4. (The) Apprentice

5. (The) Brady Bunch

6. Cone Heads

7. Extreme Makeover

8. General Hospital

9. I Love Lucy

10. Little House on the Prairie

11. Nightline

12. Pelican Brief

13. Pet Cemetery

14. Peter Pan

15. Popeye

16. Real World

17. Sixth Sense

18. South Park

19. Spiderman

20. SpongeBob SquarePants

21. Star Trek

22. Survivor

23. Titanic

24. Wheel of Fortune

entertainment

Category	Entertainment
1	9 to 5
Rating	Intermediate to Difficult

Description "9 to 5" is a humorous movie starring Dolly Parton, Lily Tomlin, and Jane Fonda about women working in an office

THE LOGIC

First Picture	A single complex picture of a clock set for 4:51
Put it all together	Another way of saying the time "51 minutes after 4 o'clock" is to say that is it "9 minutes before 5 o'clock" or "9 to 5"

COMMON MISCONCEPTIONS

1. This is a very hard picture word because there are several levels of assumptions that must occur to solve the puzzle.

2. Most people could probably solve this puzzle if it were not a digital clock, because then it is more apparent that it is 9 minutes before 5 o'clock. But with a digital clock, the connection just doesn't happen. Players sit there and say "four fifty-one" or "fifty-one minutes after four" over and over again.

entertainment

Category	Entertainment
2	101 Dalmatians
Rating	Easy to Intermediate

Description "101 Dalmatians" is a Walt Disney movie about the lives of a group of Dalmatians

THE LOGIC

First Picture	The letters "CI," which are Roman numerals for 101
Second Picture	A picture of two Dalmatians
Put it all together	CI + Dalmatians or 101 Dalmatians

COMMON MISCONCEPTIONS

1. This is easy if you know your Roman numerals. If not, this just became a very difficult puzzle. (Usually someone in the group knows Roman numerals.)

2. Most people know that a Dalmatian is a dog with lots of spots, so they guess this first and then work backward.

Category	Entertainment
3	Addams Family
Rating	Easy

Description "The Addams Family" is an old comedy show from the seventies about a strange family who live in a large castle; each member of the family has a different and unique ghoulish characteristic

THE LOGIC

First Picture	A picture of three spinning atoms
Second Picture	A picture of a small family
Put it all together	atoms family or Addams Family

COMMON MISCONCEPTIONS

1. This is a relatively easy combination of two simple words.

entertainment

Learn-o-grams™. Copyright © 2007 by John Wiley & Sons, Inc. Reproduced by permission of Pfeiffer, an Imprint of Wiley. www.pfeiffer.com

Category	Entertainment
4	(The) Apprentice
Rating	Intermediate to Difficult

Description "The Apprentice" is a very popular TV show starring Donald Trump, who gives working people a series of challenges to overcome

THE LOGIC

First Picture	An ape
Second Picture	A sign that indicates apartment for rent
Third Picture	A small block of ice
Put it all together	ape + rent + ice or "apprentice"

COMMON MISCONCEPTIONS

1. Players think that the ape is a "monkey" or a "baboon" or a "guerilla." For some reason, the word "ape" is less common, and this presents more complexity for finding the solution.

2. "Apartment available" is another phrase that really throws people off-track. Players just say it over and over again without thinking of the other implications such that, if an apartment is available, it is also "for rent."

3. The block of ice is usually the simplest part of the puzzle and often the starting point for solving this deceptively tough picture word.

Learn-o-grams™

Learn-o-grams™. Copyright © 2007 by John Wiley & Sons, Inc. Reproduced by permission of Pfeiffer, an Imprint of Wiley. www.pfeiffer.com

Category	Entertainment
5	(The) Brady Bunch
Rating	Easy to Intermediate

Description "The Brady Bunch" was a humorous TV show in the sixties about a large blended family with three girls and three boys and their silly antics

THE LOGIC

First Picture	A single complex picture: (1) A bunch of bananas and (2) Several sets of braided hair attached to the bananas
Put it all together	braids + bunch or "braided bunch" or Brady Bunch

COMMON MISCONCEPTIONS

1. Everyone gets the bunch of bananas right away.

2. The braids are more difficult for players to figure out, but not that hard.

3. However, making the leap to the braided bunch of bananas and thus "The Brady Bunch" is a little more complex. This puzzle is very age-sensitive and often requires team effort.

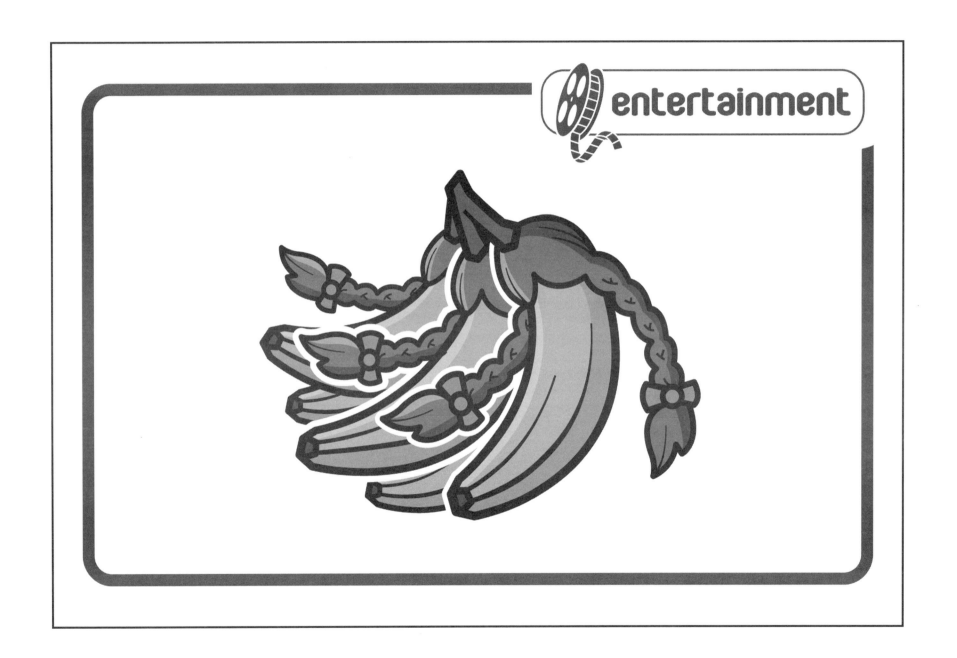

Learn-o-grams™. Copyright © 2007 by John Wiley & Sons, Inc. Reproduced by permission of Pfeiffer, an Imprint of Wiley. www.pfeiffer.com

Category	Entertainment
6	Cone Heads
Rating	Easy

Description "Cone Heads" is a fun movie about a family from another planet that crash lands on earth during a trip and how they adapt to life on this planet

THE LOGIC

First Picture	A cone for ice cream
Second Picture	Two quarters with their "heads" side facing up
Put it all together	cone + heads or "Cone Heads"

COMMON MISCONCEPTIONS

1. The cone is very simple to guess.

2. The "heads" are more difficult because people say, "two quarters," "two coins," "money," or "change" and have a hard time isolating the simple word "heads."

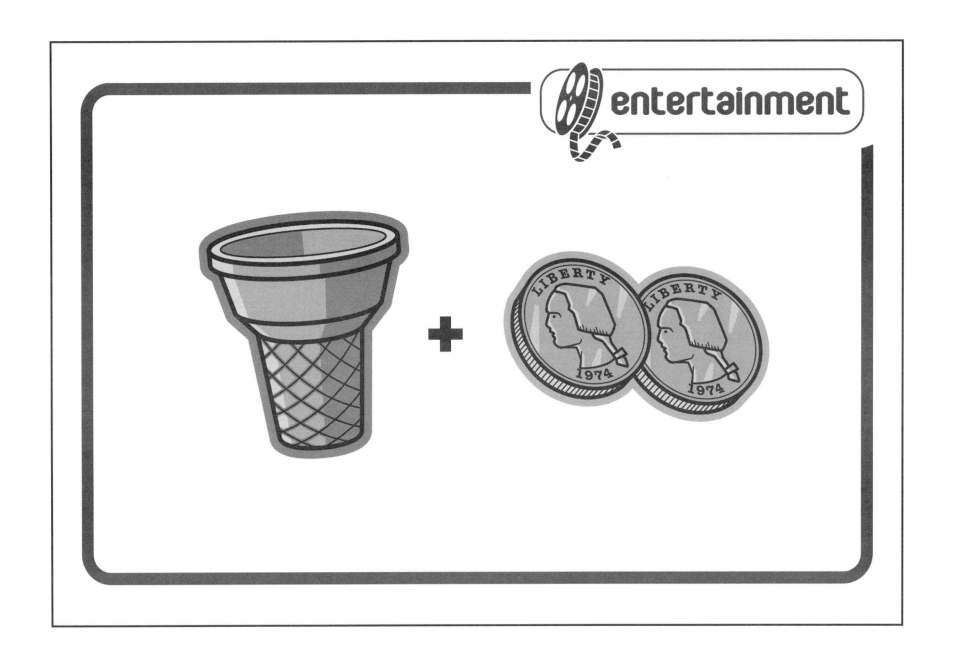

Learn-o-grams™. Copyright © 2007 by John Wiley & Sons, Inc. Reproduced by permission of Pfeiffer, an Imprint of Wiley. www.pfeiffer.com

Category	Entertainment
7	Extreme Makeover
Rating	Intermediate to Difficult

Description "Extreme Makeover" is a TV show that started out as a program about plastic surgery, then branched out into a second show on which they completely renovate or rebuild someone's house from top to bottom

THE LOGIC

First Picture | A single complex picture: (1) The word "make" over (2) A division sign or a platform with (3) A river or stream running between some trees with a bunch of "X's" floating down it

Put it all together | A river or stream running with a bunch of "X's" floating on it below the word "make" with a division sign between them or the word "make" over a stream with X's (X stream) or "X stream make over" or "Extreme Makeover"

COMMON MISCONCEPTIONS

1. This is a very difficult puzzle to solve because it is very abstract and complex due to the positions of the items in it.

2. The stream is confused with a "river," a "brook," or a "tributary" and no one ever can figure out why the "X's" are floating down it and that it is an "X stream."

3. The "X stream" is under the word "make" or the word "make" is over the "X stream," depending on how you look at it.

Learn-o-grams™. Copyright © 2007 by John Wiley & Sons, Inc. Reproduced by permission of Pfeiffer, an Imprint of Wiley. www.pfeiffer.com

Category	Entertainment
8	General Hospital
Rating	Easy

Description "General Hospital" is a long-running soap opera about the complex lives of doctors and nurses who work in a hospital

THE LOGIC

First Picture — A "General" in the military

Second Picture — A building with a large red cross on the top indicating an emergency landing zone, thus a hospital

Put it all together — Simply general and hospital or "General Hospital"

COMMON MISCONCEPTIONS

1. This is a very easy picture word and usually there are no misconceptions.

entertainment

Category	Entertainment
9	I Love Lucy
Rating	Easy

Description "I Love Lucy" is a famous TV show from the fifties about the zany adventures of Lucille Ball and Desi Arnez and their life together

THE LOGIC

First Picture	An eye
Second Picture	A heart denoting love
Third Picture	The letter "C" with the name "Lou" on it
Put it all together	eye + love + Lou's C or "I love Lucy"

COMMON MISCONCEPTIONS

1. The eye and the heart are relatively easy to decipher.

2. The "C" with the word "Lou" in front of it takes a minute, but most players figure out the combination of the Lou C very quickly.

entertainment

Learn-o-grams™. Copyright © 2007 by John Wiley & Sons, Inc. Reproduced by permission of Pfeiffer, an Imprint of Wiley. www.pfeiffer.com

Category	Entertainment
10	Little House on the Prairie
Rating	Intermediate

Description "Little House on the Prairie" is a classic TV show from the sixties and seventies about a large family living in the rugged frontier of the Western United States and all their trials and joys

THE LOGIC

First Picture	A single complex picture: (1) A small or "little" house, (2) The letter e, and (3) Praying hands extending from the letter e
Put it all together	A little house sitting on top of the letter e, which is in fact alive and praying or "little house on the prayer e" or "Little House on the Prairie"

COMMON MISCONCEPTIONS

1. A great deal of difficulty occurs in trying to put this whole picture together. People see the house and the letter e right away, but can't put it all together.

2. Once they figure out that the e is praying, it is still difficult to convert it to a "prayer E" or "prairie."

Learn-o-grams™

Learn-o-grams™. Copyright © 2007 by John Wiley & Sons, Inc. Reproduced by permission of Pfeiffer, an Imprint of Wiley. www.pfeiffer.com

Description "Nightline" is a news show that appears on TV regularly late at night

THE LOGIC

First Picture	A knight in full armor
Second Picture	A fishing rod with its fishing line intact and an arrow pointing at the line
Put it all together	A knight and a fishing line or "knight line" or "Nightline"

COMMON MISCONCEPTIONS

1. The knight is easy to recognize, but many times people can't easily think of what this is called and say, "man in armor" or "warrior."

2. The fishing rod is a little more difficult because there are many options to choose from. Players say "fishing rod," "fishing pole," and then finally "fishing line."

entertainment

Category	Entertainment
12	Pelican Brief
Rating	Easy to Intermediate

Description *Pelican Brief* is a famous novel by John Grisham about the corruption of lawyers, made into a movie

THE LOGIC

First Picture	A single complex picture: (1) A pelican that is (2) Wearing briefs
Put it all together	Pelican wearing briefs or "Pelican Brief"

COMMON MISCONCEPTIONS

1. In the absence of knowing the movie, the logic in this picture doesn't make much sense.

2. Players say that this is a "seagull" or a "large bird," but have a little trouble figuring out that it is a pelican.

3. Players guess that the bird is wearing "underwear," "shorts," or "boxers" at first, and only after a few trials think of the word "briefs."

entertainment

Learn-o-grams™. Copyright © 2007 by John Wiley & Sons, Inc. Reproduced by permission of Pfeiffer, an Imprint of Wiley. www.pfeiffer.com

Category	Entertainment
13	Pet Cemetery
Rating	Intermediate to Difficult
Description	"Pet Cemetery" is a well-known horror movie

THE LOGIC

First Picture	A bunch of tombstones in a cemetery
Second Picture	Every tombstone has an animal's name on it and the dates that they lived
Put it all together	A cemetery for pets or "Pet Cemetery"

COMMON MISCONCEPTIONS

1. Everyone knows this is a cemetery, but connecting the fact that pets are there is difficult for even the smartest.

2. Only by thinking outside the box and reading exactly what is on the fronts of the tombstones can players realize that this cemetery is for pets.

Category	Entertainment
14	Peter Pan
Rating	Easy

Description "Peter Pan" is a famous children's movie about a boy who can fly and doesn't want to grow up

THE LOGIC

First Picture	A pea
Second Picture	A person tearing a piece of paper
Third Picture	A frying pan with two eggs in it
Put it all together	pea + tearing paper + a pan or "pea tear pan" or "Peter Pan"

COMMON MISCONCEPTIONS

1. This is a relatively easy puzzle because each piece is easy to recognize.

2. Sometimes participants have trouble with the tearing paper and call it a "rip" or a "break."

3. Players have trouble figuring out "pan" and call it a "pot" or say "frying."

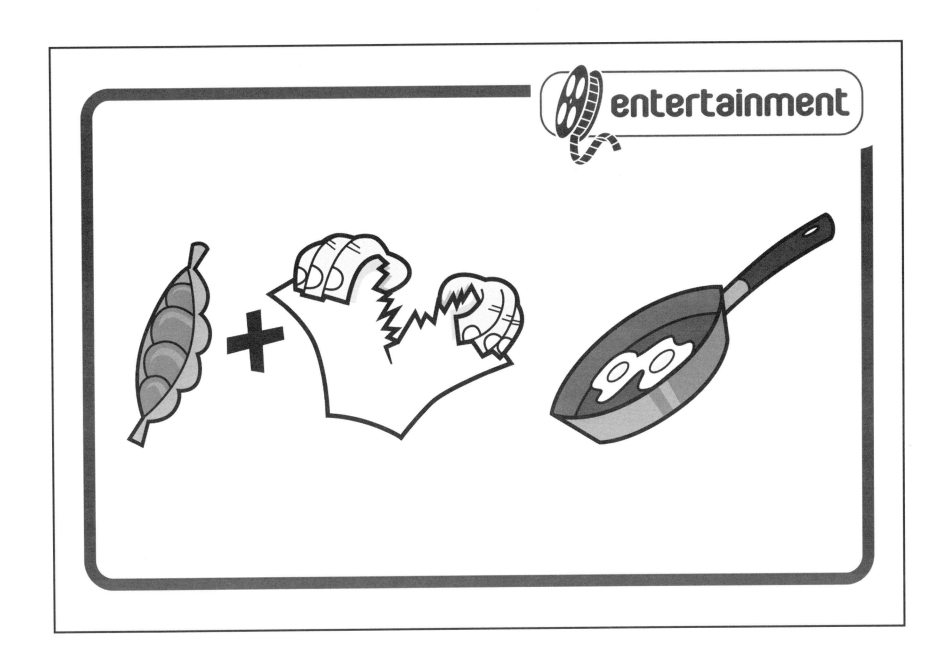

Learn-o-grams™. Copyright © 2007 by John Wiley & Sons, Inc. Reproduced by permission of Pfeiffer, an Imprint of Wiley. www.pfeiffer.com

Category	Entertainment
15	Popeye
Rating	Easy

Description Popeye is a well-known cartoon character known for the strength he receives after he eats spinach

THE LOGIC

First Picture	A bottle of soda or "pop"
Second Picture	An eye
Put it all together	pop + eye or Popeye

COMMON MISCONCEPTIONS

1. A very easy puzzle, good to start out with.

2. One problem with the bottle of soda occurs because people from different regions do not know the word "pop."

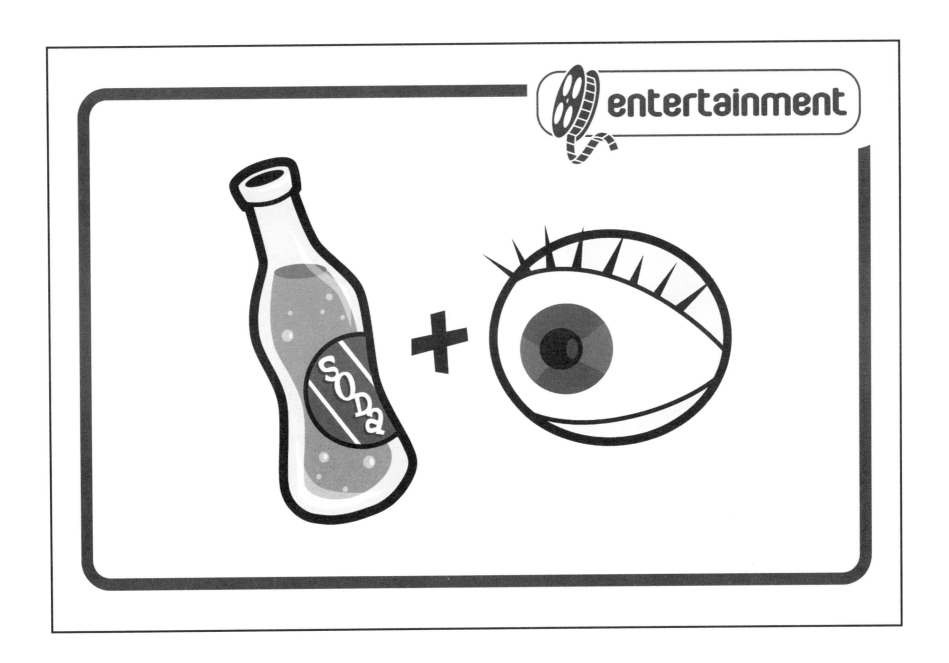

entertainment

Category	Entertainment
16	Real World
Rating	Easy to Intermediate

Description   "Real World" is a teenage-based reality show filming young adults and their interactions while living together in the real world

THE LOGIC

First Picture	A fishing reel
Second Picture	A panoramic view of the earth or "world"
Put it all together	reel + world or "Real World"

COMMON MISCONCEPTIONS

1. A relatively easy puzzle, but only if the person guessing is younger and knows of the show.

2. Additionally, people say "fishing rod" over and over again and can't figure out that it is actually a "reel."

3. The "world" is relatively easy to get.

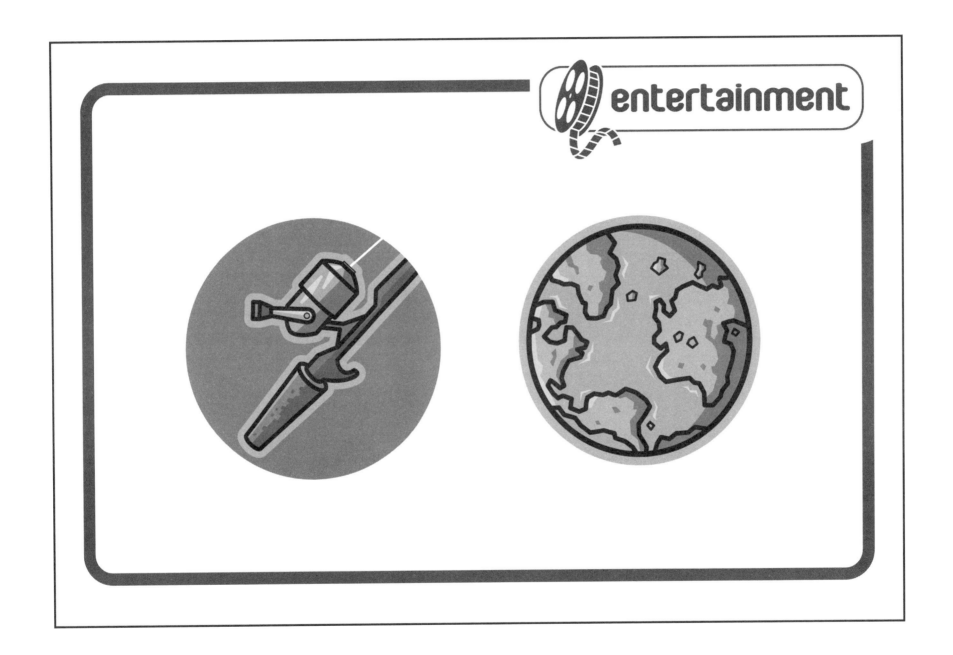

Category	Entertainment
17	Sixth Sense
Rating	Intermediate to Difficult

Description "The Sixth Sense" is a great science fiction mystery movie about a boy who can see the dead and his experiences

THE LOGIC

First Picture — Six pennies in a row or "six cents"

Second Picture — The sixth cent is turned over to denote that it is of special importance

Put it all together — There are several "cents" and the sixth one is highlighted so word one is "sixth"; there are a number of pennies or cents, so combining them you have "the sixth cent" or "The Sixth Sense"

COMMON MISCONCEPTIONS

1. People get hung up on the simple word "cents" and continue to call these denomination of money "pennies."

2. It is difficult to tie together the abstract concepts into one answer. There are actually many interpretations of the picture word, and the connections are not easy to make. If one is familiar with the movie, then it is easier.

<table>
<tr><td>Category</td><td>Entertainment</td></tr>
<tr><td>18</td><td>South Park</td></tr>
<tr><td>Rating</td><td>Easy</td></tr>
</table>

Description "South Park" is a humorous but dry and cynical cartoon show about political satire

THE LOGIC

First Picture	A wind vane facing south
Second Picture	An automatic gear shifter in a car in the "park" position
Put it all together	south + park or "South Park"

COMMON MISCONCEPTIONS

1. People don't think about the different directions on the wind vane and say "vane," "wind," and all the directions. But this wind vane is pointing south.

2. Many people have a hard time figuring out that this is a gear shift in a car with the gear set for P or "park."

3. This is especially difficult for those from a big city, where people often don't own cars.

Learn-o-grams™. Copyright © 2007 by John Wiley & Sons, Inc. Reproduced by permission of Pfeiffer, an Imprint of Wiley. www.pfeiffer.com

Category	Entertainment
19	Spiderman
Rating	Easy to Intermediate

Description "Spiderman" is a fairly recent movie based on one of the legendary superheroes of Marvel comics who is capable of transporting himself almost anywhere, defying gravity by using his web-like projectiles (just like a spider)

THE LOGIC

First Picture	A pie with an S in the middle
Second Picture	A door
Third Picture	A man
Put it all together	A pie with an S or S + pie, with a door and a man or S + pie + door + man or Spiderman

COMMON MISCONCEPTIONS

1. This one takes a little thinking because many players say "pie S" or "pies" or "pie man's" and then finally get "S + pie."

2. Once players get the first part or complete the last section, the puzzle is very easy.

Learn-o-grams™

Category	Entertainment
20	SpongeBob SquarePants
Rating	Easy

Description SpongeBob SquarePants is a surreal, funny-looking cartoon character on a TV show for little children

THE LOGIC

First Picture	A sponge in the shape of the word "Bob"
Second Picture	A square
Third Picture	A pair of pants
Put it all together	sponge Bob + square + pants or SpongeBob SquarePants

COMMON MISCONCEPTIONS

1. Some players say the word "Bob" first or "Bob wet sponge" or "Bob sponge."

2. Players also say "square jeans."

3. Once players get any one of these pieces, they put it all together very quickly.

Category	Entertainment
21	Star Trek
Rating	Intermediate to Difficult

Description "Star Trek" is the famous show and movie starring Captain Kirk, Dr. Spock, and the adventures of the USS Enterprise, on TV for many years and spun off into movies starring the same cast

THE LOGIC

First Picture	A star with arms and legs walking or "trekking"
Second Picture	The entire scene is on a mountainside
Put it all together	A star that is walking or "trekking" up the side of a mountain or "Star Trek"

COMMON MISCONCEPTIONS

1. The star walking is easy to guess.

2. Figuring out that a walk becomes a "trek" when you are going up the steep edge of a mountain is much more difficult. People say "star hike" or "star walk."

entertainment

Category	Entertainment
22	Survivor
Rating	Easy to Intermediate

Description "Survivor" is a popular TV show on which contestants must accomplish complex tasks in different harsh environments each week to beat other teams and win the grand prize

THE LOGIC

First Picture	A man on a surfboard
Second Picture	A beehive
Third Picture	An oar
Put it all together	surf + hive + oar or "survivor"

COMMON MISCONCEPTIONS

1. Each individual part of this picture word puzzle is relatively easy to identify.

2. The beehive is difficult for some people, who say "bees," "honey," "wasp," "stingers," and so on, missing the word "hive."

3. The difficulty is getting the sound-alike. Many people just keep saying the words "surf hive oar" over and over again, and it doesn't click. Often someone else listening hears it and the words jump out at them in a big surprise.

Category	Entertainment
23	Titanic
Rating	Easy

Description "Titanic" was a movie about the doomed voyage of one of the most famous ocean liners of all time, which sank after hitting an iceberg on its maiden voyage

THE LOGIC

First Picture	A person wearing a tie
Second Picture	A person getting a suntan
Third Picture	Someone's neck
Put it all together	tie + tan + neck or Titanic

COMMON MISCONCEPTIONS

1. A simple puzzle with three easy parts to guess.

Learn-o-grams™. Copyright © 2007 by John Wiley & Sons, Inc. Reproduced by permission of Pfeiffer, an Imprint of Wiley. www.pfeiffer.com

THE LOGIC

First Picture	A single complex picture: (1) A standard automobile tire or a wheel on which (2) The spokes are made up of four 2,000-pound weights (each one is a ton)
Put it all together	A tire or wheel that has spokes made out of four 2,000-pound weights, or a wheel made out of four one-ton weights, or "wheel of four tons," or "Wheel of Fortune"

COMMON MISCONCEPTIONS

1. Everyone guesses "tire" right away but they often have a hard time figuring out that it is a wheel.

2. Even though most people know that the weights in the middle are tons, it is very difficult for people to grasp the unlikely connection between the wheel and the tons. It is even harder to connect the fact that there are four one-ton spokes.

3. Last, it is hard for people to get the sound-alike of "four tons" and "fortune."

Learn-o-grams™

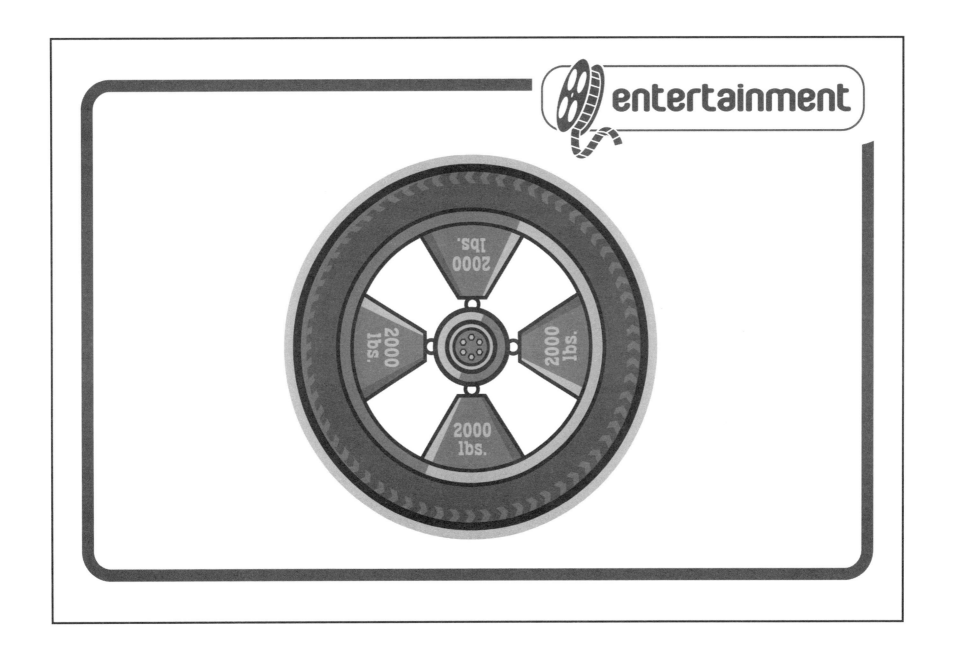

Picture Words: Clichés

On the next page is an alphabetical list of the twenty-four Cliché cards (a famous saying or quote with a deeper meaning) that corresponds to the full-page picture words on the right-hand pages in this chapter.

Overall Level of Difficulty of This Category: Intermediate to Very Difficult

Clichés are the most difficult category because they are almost always abstract, have an alternative meaning, and can be extremely generation-based. However, that being said, one who gains mastery over the art of

Learn-o-grams™ should have no problem solving these Cliché puzzles.

EACH LEFT-HAND PAGE CONTAINS

1. A description of the Learn-o-gram™ sketch

2. An explanation of the logic for each segment of the picture to make it easier to explain the answers

3. A comment on common misconceptions that occur when typical participants try to solve the Learn-o-grams™

1. Ace in the hole
2. Back to square one
3. Breaking the ice
4. The buck stops here
5. A burning question
6. Called on the carpet
7. Compare apples to oranges
8. Cut a long story short
9. Dog eat dog
10. Don't beat around the bush
11. A drop in the bucket
12. Go for broke

13. Half-baked idea
14. I have a bone to pick
15. Lock, stock, and barrel
16. Loose cannon
17. No spring chicken
18. Not under any circumstances
19. On a rampage
20. One foot in the grave
21. Pass the buck
22. Rat race
23. Read between the lines
24. Sign of the times

CLICHES

Category	Clichés
1	Ace in the Hole
Rating	Intermediate

Description Having an "ace in the hole" is saying that you have a back-up plan, a special or secret resource to help you out of a sticky situation or a hidden tool that others don't know about

THE LOGIC

First Picture | A single complex picture: (1) A big hole in the ground and (2) A bunch of "A's" facing all different directions

Put it all together | A big hole with a bunch of A's, or A's in the hole, or "ace in the hole"

COMMON MISCONCEPTIONS

1. Players will have a hard time realizing that a bunch of "A's" really could be the word "ace." They will probably say the word "A's" over and over again.

2. A major complexity in this Learn-o-gram™ is trying to figure out what the relationship is between the A's and the hole. Because everyone thinks it is funny, almost every person older than around thirteen misconstrues the answer and puts together the letters "A" and the world "hole" to make an inappropriate profane word. Talk about preconceived notions, this one is very ingrained into almost all adults. However funny it is, participants have a hard time tying the two parts of this picture word together to get the answer.

THE LOGIC

First Picture	A person's back
Second Picture	Two squares
Third Picture	The number "1" written in both squares
Put it all together	A person's back and two squares with 1's in them or "back two square one" or "back to square one"

COMMON MISCONCEPTIONS

1. A relatively easy puzzle because each individual piece is easy to identify.

2. It is a little difficult to get the right order of the "to square one" portion. Players say "back squares one in each" or "back 2 square number one."

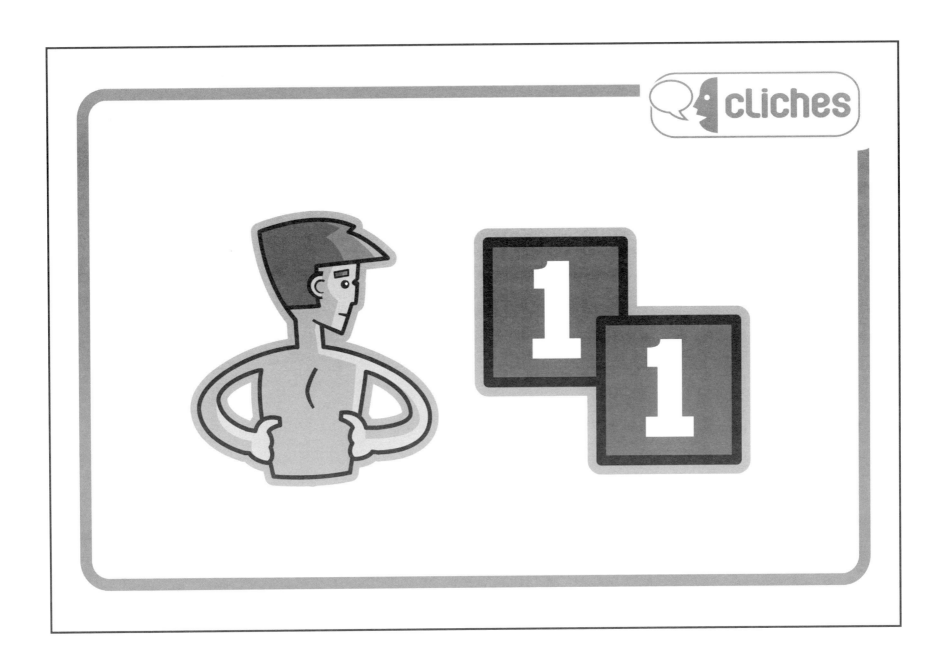

Category	Clichés
3	Breaking the Ice
Rating	Intermediate to Difficult

Description "Breaking the ice" refers to helping people in social situations to relax more and be less anxious, especially in the first few minutes of meeting one another

THE LOGIC

First Picture	A single complex picture: (1) A bunch of "I's" of different sizes and shapes and (2) A hammer breaking all the I's apart
Put it all together	A hammer breaking apart a bunch of different shaped and sized "I's" or "breaking the I's" or "breaking the ice"

COMMON MISCONCEPTIONS

1. This phrase is very difficult for most people, as they focus on the hammer and the subsequent apparent explosion, rather than on the letters themselves.

Players first just sit there dumbfounded and say nothing. Once they study the picture, players say things like "hammering the I," "I explosion" or "breaking an I." After a while, they figure out that there are several I's and finally say "hammering" or "breaking the I's."

2. Trying to convert the multiple "I's" to the word "ice" is very difficult visually. However, this is one case in which a team member who is a strong auditory learner will be very valuable. If one team member is saying "breaking the I's" and another team member hears these words, he or she will easily be able to convert it to the word "ice" because it sounds like that. The transition between a bunch of "I's" and the word "ice" is simple for our ears, but very difficult for our eyes.

Learn-o-grams™. Copyright © 2007 by John Wiley & Sons, Inc. Reproduced by permission of Pfeiffer, an Imprint of Wiley. www.pfeiffer.com

Category   Clichés

4   The Buck Stops Here

Rating   Intermediate

Description "The buck stops here" means the responsibility for any actions or behaviors that have occurred stop with a particular person or team or unit—specifically, this phrase means that one person is admitting that he or she is responsible for whatever happened

THE LOGIC

First Picture   A dollar bill (or a "buck," slang for a dollar) driving a car

Second Picture   The car is at a stop sign

Put it all together Literally, the dollar bill is required to stop at the stop sign or "the buck stops here"

COMMON MISCONCEPTIONS

1. All the components of this picture are crystal-clear, but the human brain works on familiar patterns and pre-conceived notions and it does not like this puzzle.

2. People say things like, "The mighty dollar drives business" or "Bill drives the car" or "The dollar must stop at the stop sign."

3. To put this Learn-o-gram™ together requires combining out-of-the-box thinking and logically seeing what is in front of you. The "buck" is driving, and it stops at a stop sign.

STOP

Category	Clichés
5	A Burning Question
Rating	Easy to Intermediate

Description "A burning question" is one that is very important to ask or discuss in a particular situation (As a college professor, I often ask my students to answer a very important "burning question" about a specific topic)

THE LOGIC

First Picture	A single complex picture: (1) A large question mark and (2) A flame engulfing the question mark
Put it all together	A question that is burning or "a burning question"

COMMON MISCONCEPTIONS

1. Although this is a simple picture, players often say "a question mark on fire" or a "hot question" or a "a flaming question."

2. It is not really difficult to connect the concept of a question with the question mark, but for some reason people's brains short-circuit when they try to combine a fire with a question mark to get "a burning question."

Category	Clichés
6	Called on the Carpet
Rating	Intermediate to Difficult

Description "Called on the carpet" means that someone is being very honest with another person about a problem regarding his or her shortcoming that must be corrected; being called on the carpet is not usually a positive experience, but one where a problem is being laid out clearly, and solutions are urgently sought after without sensitivity to the listener's emotions or feelings

THE LOGIC

First Picture	A single complex picture: (1) A person sitting on a flying carpet and (2) A person on the telephone, perhaps receiving a call
Put it all together	A person receiving a call while sitting on a carpet or being called while on the carpet or "called on the carpet"

COMMON MISCONCEPTIONS

1. This Learn-o-gram™ is difficult because players cannot make the connection between riding on a carpet and receiving a phone call.

2. Players have a hard time putting these two simple concepts together. Additionally, players find thinking in the past tense very difficult.

3. They say "carpet call" or "flying carpet call" or "flying call." Interestingly enough, when asked, players always tell me that the carpet rider is actually making an *outgoing* call.

Picture Words: Clichés

Learn-o-grams™. Copyright © 2007 by John Wiley & Sons, Inc. Reproduced by permission of Pfeiffer, an Imprint of Wiley. www.pfeiffer.com

Category	Clichés
7	Compare Apples to Oranges
Rating	Easy

Description If one "compares apples to oranges" when evaluating two different components of any system, the implication is that the items may not really be similar (although both are fruit, apples and oranges are very different)

THE LOGIC

First Picture	A convict or "con"
Second Picture	A pear
Third Picture	An apple with an "S" on it
Fourth Picture	Two oranges
Put it all together	Con + pear + apple + s + two oranges or "compare apples to oranges"

COMMON MISCONCEPTIONS

1. This Learn-o-gram™ is very straightforward and most people have heard this cliché.

Learn-o-grams™. Copyright © 2007 by John Wiley & Sons, Inc. Reproduced by permission of Pfeiffer, an Imprint of Wiley. www.pfeiffer.com

Category	Clichés
8	Cut a Long Story Short
Rating	Intermediate

Description "Cut a long story short" really means to get to the point and to be more succinct and focused in your discussion

THE LOGIC

First Picture

A single complex picture: (1) A picture of a very thick book, *War and Peace,* a very long and drawn-out story and (2) A scissors cutting the book

Put it all together

A long drawn-out story is being cut in half or cutting a long story in half or "cut a long story short"

COMMON MISCONCEPTIONS

1. This is a little difficult because players focus on the book and its title rather than the thickness and thus the length of the story.

2. The scissors is key, but because it is cutting the book horizontally instead of right through the middle of the book, the answer is hidden.

3. Players say "cutting a book in half" or "telling half the story" or "a short story," but have a hard time connecting the entire cliché.

Category	Clichés
9	Dog Eat Dog
Rating	Easy

Description "Dog eat dog" is a phrase that denotes the harshness of the world that we live in; "It's a dog-eat-dog world" means that sometimes it is a battle to survive and that only the strong and aggressive come out on top

THE LOGIC

First Picture	A single complex picture: (1) A big, friendly dog who is (2) eating a hot dog
Put it all together	The phrase shows literally what is going on in the picture, "a dog eating a hot dog," or more simply, "dog eat dog"

COMMON MISCONCEPTIONS

1. A very simple and humorous puzzle that most people figure out quickly.

Category	Clichés
10	Don't Beat Around the Bush
Rating	Difficult

Description "Don't beat around the bush" means "Just get to the point" or "Let's get on the task at hand"

THE LOGIC

First Picture	A bunch of beets in a square formation
Second Picture	A bush in the middle
Third Picture	The "no" or "do not" sign from traffic control
Put it all together	A bunch of beets are around a bush, and all of them are surrounded by the "no" or "do not" sign; thus, there are beets around the bush with the "no" or "do not" sign or "Don't beat around the bush"

COMMON MISCONCEPTIONS

1. The trick to this Learn-o-gram™ is to understand how all the pieces tie together. In this puzzle, the location of the beets in relation to the bush is very significant, just as the "do not" or "no" frame surrounding the beets gives it a totally different meaning. What makes this puzzle so hard is that there are many possible combinations.

Category	Clichés
11	A Drop in the Bucket
Rating	Easy to Intermediate

Description "A drop in the bucket" refers to the comparative size of any project, object, or task at hand; to say that it is "a drop in the bucket" denotes that this is only a small portion of the required effort or resources or assets necessary to complete a task or project

THE LOGIC

First Picture	A drop of water
Second Picture	A pin
Third Picture	A dollar bill or "buck"
Fourth Picture	A cat
Put it all together	Just as it appears phonetically, a drop + pin + buck + cat or "a drop in the bucket"

COMMON MISCONCEPTIONS

1. A very simple, fun, straightforward puzzle.

2. To solve this one, it is necessary to get the fact that buck + cat sounds like "bucket."

Learn-o-grams™. Copyright © 2007 by John Wiley & Sons, Inc. Reproduced by permission of Pfeiffer, an Imprint of Wiley. www.pfeiffer.com

Category   Clichés

12   Go for Broke

Rating   Easy

Description "Go for broke" means take a big risk or risk everything or throw caution to the wind

THE LOGIC

First Picture   A gopher

Second Picture   A stick that is broken

Put it all together gopher + a broken stick or "go for broke"

COMMON MISCONCEPTIONS

1. One difficult part of this puzzle is getting the concept of the broken stick connected to a stick that is already broken or "broke."

2. Some people think the animal is a groundhog instead of a gopher.

Picture Words: Clichés   *Learn-o-grams™*. Copyright © 2007 by John Wiley & Sons, Inc. Reproduced by permission of Pfeiffer, an Imprint of Wiley. www.pfeiffer.com

Category	Clichés
13	Half-Baked Idea
Rating	Intermediate to Difficult

Description   A "half-baked idea" is one that is zany or crazy or "out of the box" and defies conventional thinking

THE LOGIC

First Picture	A loaf of bread that is only half there and is baking
Second Picture	A man with a lightbulb going off, signaling a great idea
Put it all together	Half a loaf of baked bread and a man who has an idea going off in his head or a half-baked loaf of bread and a great idea or "a half-baked idea"

COMMON MISCONCEPTIONS

1. This is difficult because of trying to figure out what is actually going on in the oven. There is only half a loaf of bread and it is being baked, so it is half-baked. People say, "a partially cooked loaf of bread," or "uncooked dough," but have difficulty with "half-baked."

2. The lightbulb is pretty easy as it denotes an idea going on in the man's head.

Category	Clichés
14	I Have a Bone to Pick
Rating	Easy to Intermediate

Description "I have a bone to pick" means the speaker is upset or disappointed and wants to talk about a situation or problem that needs to be discussed urgently

THE LOGIC

First Picture	An eye
Second Picture	A beehive
Third Picture	A bone
Fourth Picture	Two large picks for digging
Put it all together	eye + hive + a bone + two picks, or "I have a bone to pick"

COMMON MISCONCEPTIONS

1. One of the easier clichés because each part of the phrase is very apparent. (There is one sound-alike: "hive" and "have.")

2. The hardest part of the picture word is simply saying the words "two picks." Most people say "pick axes" or "two big picks" or "picks."

Category	Clichés
15	Lock, Stock, and Barrel
Rating	Easy to Intermediate

Description "Lock, stock, and barrel" is an old saying that means that you are completely committed or involved and giving 100 percent of your effort or resources

THE LOGIC

First Picture	A lock
Second Picture	Two steers or oxen
Third Picture	A barrel
Put it all together	A lock, two livestock or "stock," and a barrel or, very simply, "lock, stock, and barrel"

COMMON MISCONCEPTIONS

1. The only issue with this Learn-o-gram™ is making the subtle connection of the two animals to being "livestock" and then to just "stock." Although this is logical, it is a bit of a stretch.

Picture Words: Clichés   *Learn-o-grams™*. Copyright © 2007 by John Wiley & Sons, Inc. Reproduced by permission of Pfeiffer, an Imprint of Wiley. www.pfeiffer.com   245

Category   Clichés

16   Loose Cannon

Rating   Intermediate

Description "A loose cannon" refers to a member of a team who is often highly unpredictable and who has very few limits and poor boundaries and does whatever he or she wants to do

THE LOGIC

First Picture   A single complex picture: (1) A picture of a cannon and (2) A sign on the cannon that says "Lou's"

Put it all together   A cannon that belongs to Lou or Lou's cannon or "loose cannon"

COMMON MISCONCEPTIONS

1. This Learn-o-gram™ has one difficult point, and that is changing your preconceived notion about the name on the cannon. This is not any ordinary cannon but one with a name on the front because it belongs to Lou.

PROPERTY OF
LOU

Category	Clichés
17	No Spring Chicken
Rating	Very Difficult

Description "No spring chicken" is a very old saying that means a person is not as young he or she used to be anymore

THE LOGIC

First Picture	A list of the months of the year that is missing several key months associated with "spring"
Second Picture	A chicken
Put it all together	If you look at the list of months and ask yourself which months are missing, you will notice that all the months associated with "spring" are not there, so there is "no spring." Combine this with the chicken and you have "no spring chicken."

COMMON MISCONCEPTIONS

1. This is a very difficult puzzle because players have to deduce what is missing from the picture in order to solve it. Only when participants realize that the months associated with "spring" are missing can they begin to grasp the concept of "no spring."

2. Once they get "no spring," then they can easily add the word "chicken" to get the answer, "no spring chicken."

Category	Clichés
18	Not Under Any Circumstances
Rating	Intermediate

Description "Not under any circumstances" means there is no chance that an action will take place

THE LOGIC

First Picture — A single complex picture: (1) The words "any circumstances," (2) A horizontal line that separates the other two items, and (3) A picture of a knot

Put it all together — The words "any circumstances" are situated just above a separating line, which is above the knot, or the knot is just below or under the words "any circumstances" or "knot" under "any circumstances" or "not under any circumstances"

COMMON MISCONCEPTIONS

1. The positioning of the two items in this picture creates significant confusion in the minds of participants. Players will say "any circumstances over the knot" or "any circumstances divided by knot" or "knot below any circumstances," but often continue to miss the simple solution that the knot is "under" the words.

any circumstances

Category	Clichés
19	On a Rampage
Rating	Easy

Description "On a rampage" means simply that the person is very angry and upset and may in fact be walking or moving around chaotically in a disgruntled mood

THE LOGIC

First Picture	A light switch in the "on" position
Second Picture	An open book with an image of a ram on the page
Put it all together	The light switch in the "on" position, plus a picture of a ram on the page of a book, or simply "on a page with a ram" or "on a ram page" or "on a rampage"

COMMON MISCONCEPTIONS

1. This is an easy set of picture words to guess individually, but it's quite tricky to put all the images together.

Category	Clichés
20	One Foot in the Grave
Rating	Easy

Description "One foot in the grave" either refers to someone who is in trouble and is already having serious problems or someone whose health is failing and seems to be so sick that he or she appears to be close to death

THE LOGIC

First Picture	A single complex picture: (1) A grave with an open hole and a headstone and (2) A 12-inch ruler or a one-foot ruler that is lying in the grave
Put it all together	A one-foot measure fully submerged in the actual grave or "one foot in the grave"

COMMON MISCONCEPTIONS

1. An easy puzzle that sounds just the way it looks.

Category	Clichés
21	Pass the Buck
Rating	Intermediate

Description The saying means that one should not pass on responsibility, but keep it oneself

THE LOGIC

First Picture — A single complex picture: (1) A picture of a car with a man inside who has just driven past (2) A buck (male deer) with large antlers

Put it all together — The man in the car is passing the buck, or very simply "pass the buck"

COMMON MISCONCEPTIONS

1. Although the images are very easy to guess, the relationship between the man and the buck is much more difficult. Players say "a man looking at a deer" or a "beautiful wildlife scene" or "a hunter checking out the deer before he kills it."

2. Very few people figure out that the man is actually "passing the buck."

Category	Clichés
22	Rat Race
Rating	Intermediate

Description "Rat race" is what many people refer to as the competitive and aggressive nature of their day-to-day existence in the business world

THE LOGIC

First Picture	A single complex picture: (1) A bunch of rodents or rats, (2) A race track, and (3) A finish line or flag
Put it all together	A bunch of rats running a race and just about to go across the finish line, or a race with some rats in it, or simply "a rat race"

COMMON MISCONCEPTIONS

1. A simple concept of rats running around a race track, but very difficult to make the simple connection.

Category	Clichés
23	Read Between the Lines
Rating	Easy

Description "Read between the lines" is a saying that indicates that the person is making inferences about the concept under discussion and that if one looks more deeply there may be more to the message than meets the eye

THE LOGIC

First Picture	Two lions
Second Picture	A person reading a book while sitting between the lions
Put it all together	Reading a book between two lions or, more directly, "read between the lines"

COMMON MISCONCEPTIONS

1. One of the easiest of the clichés, with no tricky concepts.

Category   Clichés

24   Sign of the Times

Rating   Intermediate to Difficult

Description   "A sign of the times" means that something has occurred that is congruent with the times that we live in or a symptom of the fact that things are changing very quickly

THE LOGIC

First Picture   A single complex picture: (1) A road sign on the side of the paved area and (2) A times table

Put it all together   A roadside sign with a times table indicating what is coming up or "a sign with a times sign on it" or "a sign of the times"

COMMON MISCONCEPTIONS

1. The pieces of this puzzle are easy to discern, but putting them together takes a good bit of trial and error. Players say "a math sign" or "a sign with a times table" or a "sign of a math problem," but have a hard time relating to a roadside sign, and seeing the obvious, which is "a sign of the times."

Conclusion

As we have seen throughout this book, playing the Learn-o-grams™ game helps people to practice thinking more creatively, outside the box, and just plain differently during the game. The objective of a training session using Learn-o-grams™ is to help players make a practical transfer of the new skills that they learn by playing this game to the workplace. Once the transfer of game-related skills is made to a broader set of work skills, the challenge is for participants to be more effective and productive. The ability to look at events, situations, and relationships differently and to see more clearly that which is apparent as well as that which is subtle and not easily discerned can be gleaned from playing Learn-o-grams™.

If playing Learn-o-grams™ can help with practicing certain key insights and transferring them to the workplace, perhaps this innocuous game can act as a tipping point to accelerate and improve performance.

Following are a few lessons from Learn-o-grams™ that can play out in any work or school setting.

●●●●●●●●●●●●●●●●●●●●●●●●●

LEARNING TO TAKE RISKS

In most business settings, people are afraid to make mistakes, so they are very cautious and careful about how much risk they take. By learning to take qualified risks, players can learn a better balance, which can lead to greater success back on the job. When people take risks and make tough decisions, they demonstrate leadership and drive innovation. In a culture that is open to taking risks, there is a positive synergy that can lead to increased productivity and exponential growth.

Playing Learn-o-grams™ can help any team be more open to and embrace risk taking.

●●●●●●●●●●●●●●●●●●●●●●●●●

PRACTICING CREATIVITY

To jump-start creativity, it is necessary to think outside of one's preconceived notions and the current environment to find new and innovative solutions. Work teams cannot learn to solve problems creatively unless they value one another's opinions and look for new ways to do things. Group brainstorming is one key to creativity. By working as a team during game play, a group can develop a new awareness of the basic creative process and make quantum leaps in their overall creativity back on the job.

"Thinking outside the box" allows participants to gain insight into the problem-solving process itself as they attempt to guess the answers and see their underlying logic.

●●●●●●●●●●●●●●●●●●●●●●●●●

ESTABLISHING A CULTURE OF TRUST AND OPENNESS

It requires a great deal of work to create a culture of trust and openness, where people are accepting enough to allow others to take the risks necessary to achieve greatness.

Learn-o-grams™ allows team members a temporary sanctuary in which to practice these skills.

Any great inventor—Edison, Ford, Einstein—made big mistakes and fell short of his goals many times before he figured out a solution. But they all had the patience and courage to move past their errors. I hope that Learn-o-grams™, as part of a program on creativity and risk taking, can serve as a trigger to help players reach a higher level of success back on the job.

Appendix

Tying the Game in to the Way People Learn

The purpose of this appendix is to give some real-life, applicable research about some of the related skills that one can gain from playing Learn-o-grams™.

THINKING DIFFERENTLY VERSUS CONFORMING

Whether it is better to think differently rather than to conform is a major area of debate in many companies. At stake is the ability to maintain a competitive edge in the international marketplace.

The dilemma is simply this: every company needs order, conformity, and obedience to maintain control. But simultaneously, the most successful companies have a focus on thinking differently, creativity, and innovation—and they have discovered that these forces drive future success.

To show the benefits for your company of using Learn-o-grams™ in your training sessions and helping people to practice the new skills that they will learn from doing so, I would like to share three of my own observations about the process:

1. Top performers all think outside the box. (This observation is based on a psychological assessment of top performers.)

2. Those who are successful make use of their *reticular activating systems* and the power of assumptions (in other words, they learn how to manage in a way that complements how their brains are wired).

3. Our mental models are crucial to the way we solve problems and our success in doing so (that is, our inborn, fixed mental models about the world affect our performance). However, we can learn to think in new ways.

Top Performers Think Differently

I sold and administered psychological assessments to hundreds of companies large and small around the country for several years. I met and assessed thousands of employees at every level—from executives to management to sales to line workers. And whether it was a behemoth Fortune 500 company or the local mom-and-pop store, one thing was always true:

> In every organization, no matter which area (management, customer service, or sales), there were always top performers and super-achievers. And all the super-achievers marched to the tune of a different drummer. Many of them (especially in sales) were quite odd and had many idiosyncrasies that set them apart.

After several years of administering the Profiles™ International personality assessments (Waco, Texas) that measured aptitude, personality, and field of interest and compared the respondent against a template of the top performers in that category, I discovered through some statistical analysis of my data that there were always three distinct segments in any company:

Top 10%	Super-achievers: extreme success, but sustainable (most of the time)
Middle 30%	Above average: good, very sustainable results (the workhorses of the organization)
Bottom 60%	Average or below-average performers: up and down, needed training, needed to be culled occasionally

Although a great deal could be said about each group, for the purpose of this discussion, I will limit my comments to the super-achievers.

The super-achievers were typically only the top 10 percent (or less). Whether in sales, management, customer service, or at the executive level, these super-performers always thought in a unique, radically different way. They also achieved unfathomable, incredible results in a sustainable and consistent manner.

After measuring these employees' capabilities for years, I came to one conclusion: This is a very difficult group to replicate. They were so contradictory to all the norms within the organization that, no matter how much testing and training a company did to try to help others to think like these high-end performers, it was usually very difficult to replicate them.

From a sales and performance point of view, this small group often produced as much business as the entire lower 50 to 60 percent of the organization. In every case I observed, the top performers' success was driven by the "far out" way they saw things and the extraordinary way they thought—just plain differently!

The quirky, strange, irrational, wacky top performers saw things in a different light. They never accepted "no" for an answer. Regardless of their intelligence levels, they were always persistent and pushed harder and harder in a relentless fashion until they achieved their desired results and maximum success. When one asked these super-achievers why they performed so well, the most common answer was something like: "Because no one said I couldn't do it!"

Playing Learn-o-grams™ can reinforce risk taking and thinking in a different way, among other traits that make super-achievers so successful.

Top Performers Make Use of the Power of Assumptions

Why do creative people make so many assumptions and continually jump to conclusions? The simple answer is that they need to fill in the many blanks in their minds and the vast gaps in their awareness. The mind searches for familiar solutions when it is unsure what to do. Because of the natural tendency of the human brain to fill in the blanks, Learn-o-grams™ can teach players how to scan the possibilities before jumping to conclusions.

Of course, everyone must make a certain number of assumptions because otherwise their conscious minds would become overloaded. If every time we needed to walk, we had to start out crawling and learn how to stand and then walk, nothing would ever get done. So we all store lots of information in our subconscious minds to make our lives easier. After we learn something (a term or a mathematical concept, for example), it comes automatically to mind when needed. We no longer have to spend a lot of time thinking about it.

The internal mechanism that controls this conscious decision-making effort is call the "reticular activating system" (RAS). The RAS filters the amount of stimuli that reaches our consciousness at any given moment. The RAS controls how we are aroused perceptually, how we direct our attention, and nerve signals to the cerebral cortex. The RAS is a great natural filtering device that helps us survive in a world of constant movement, change, and over-stimulation. It prioritizes what is important and allows that information in at the moment, thus limiting the amount of visual, auditory, and tactile stimuli and input that we receive (so that we don't go crazy from over-stimulation).

Here is an example:

A member of my family just bought a bright red Saab four-door convertible. She reports that since that purchase she has been seeing people driving Saabs everywhere she goes. Were there a lot of Saabs just sold in our area? No, her RAS has been at work, allowing a heightened sensitivity to this type of vehicle.

But the good news is that your ability to see things is not set in stone. You can train yourself to see more clearly and effectively. Playing Learn-o-grams™ can teach you how to see things more clearly during the game and to transfer other skills to your repertoire. Whether it is learning to see the big picture and the overall frame of reference or learning to focus on the here-and-now, rehearsing these skills with Learn-o-grams™ will help you to be more sensitive to your environment.

Top Performers Use New Mental Models

"Thinking outside the box" is one of the most popular buzz phrases of all time. It means thinking in ways that no one else has thought of before—outside of oneself and the familiar environment. Being creative and seeking new and original solutions to complex problems are ways to think outside the box.

The "box" is the perceptual container that holds us in our existing patterns of thought—all of our preconceived notions, ideas, and awarenesses that lock us into doing things the way they always have been done. Thinking inside the box means being safe and not having to take risks. But it also means being stuck in the same old traditional rut. Even if their attempts to solve problems haven't worked in the past, people continue to make the identical effort again and again because they see no other alternatives.

The box is filled with preconceptions of how things "should" be done by mental models, images that you have built in your head based on your own logic about the way something works. Mental models thrive on the status quo. Fear of change and the power of conformity hold people and their mental models in place.

To overcome fixed mental models, you must step back and look at the process you are using. You must question the obvious and see what is not so apparent. You must basically challenge everything you see and do. You must test your perceptions and make sure that they match the reality that you are dealing with. Just as when playing the game of Learn-o-grams™ you must question every aspect of what you see in order to solve the puzzle, you must challenge each and every "reality" that you deal with.

Edison tried over eleven hundred combinations of metals before he figured out that tungsten was the only element that would work for the lightbulb filament. He refused to be limited by what had happened before and what was "possible." When others were telling him that he had already wasted time testing five hundred elements, he said, "Every time we test a new element, we get one step closer to finding the solution."

● ●

CREATIVITY AND INNOVATION

With the pressures of the modern business world and international competition breathing down the backs of most companies, the ability to think outside the box, be creative, and constantly innovate is in high demand. Those who have mastered these skills are usually quick to rise through the ranks into leadership roles, no matter the type of business. The most successful companies are the ones with the most creative leaders.

In my consulting work, I have been asked more and more to help companies gain an upper edge in creative problem solving, creativity, innovation—and in their strategic planning. Companies are more willing than ever to take bigger risks to achieve profitable results. So the demand for learning how to use the organization's own creativity is skyrocketing.

Learn-o-grams™ helps people improve their creativity and innovation and go beyond their preconceived notions and mental models in two clear ways:

By Using the Power of Trial-and-Error Thinking

To achieve greater levels of creativity in the workplace, trial-and-error thinking must be used. The game helps participants experience the power of learning by trial and error in an open environment. Participants receive feedback on how they are performing as they go through each puzzle as team members share their thoughts and results by talking openly.

By Creating a Culture of Openness and Trust

The Learn-o-grams™ game allows players to make "appropriate, growth-related" mistakes in front of one another and encourages them to learn from the mistakes of others. In fact, many times, by hearing someone say the wrong answer, a player jumps to the correct answer. This is an excellent example of how creative groups can be when they work together. Such an open culture can accelerate the power of creativity in any organization.

I hope that these observations will help you as you debrief your own learning games and relate what happens to the work world for your participants. The effectiveness of this great game, Learn-o-grams™, is unequaled.

About the Author

Ron Roberts is president of Action Centered Training, Inc., in Eagleville, Pennsylvania, near Valley Forge, and does training, assessment, coaching, consulting, and extensive writing about experiential learning. He has invented over fifty big and small games and holds six patents, all centered around experiential learning and training. Mr. Roberts uses games to teach executives, managers, line staff, government and military, students, learning disabled and gifted students, as well as teachers, about communication, teamwork, leadership, conflict management, stress reduction, strategic planning, change management, process improvement, systems thinking, and many other soft skills.

Mr. Roberts has a master's degree in counseling psychology and owned and directed a counseling center for twelve years, where he specialized in family systems counseling (his introduction to systems thinking), testing, and assessment. He is an adjunct professor at Pennsylvania State University, Berks, and has taught organizational communication, leadership, negotiation, management competencies, and public speaking.

Professor Roberts has appeared on CNN Live and on local affiliates of ABC and NBC in Arizona, where he challenged members of MENSA. Professor Roberts has been cited in *Newsweek* and *Games* magazine as a result of winning the prestigious Dr. Toy and Parents' Choice awards. He has appeared on the QVC shopping network to demonstrate several of his inventions.

Professor Roberts invented many nationally recognized award-winning board and card games that are licensed and sold around the world. He is currently working on several new games, completing a humorous self-help book about humility and successful relationships, and is in the process of starting a new business-related manuscript on the power of humility in leadership.

How to Use the CD-ROM

WHAT'S ON THE CD-ROM

The CD-ROM contains all of the Learn-o-grams™ in executable PowerPoint™ files, with and without solutions.

SYSTEM REQUIREMENTS

PC with Microsoft Windows 98SE or later
Mac with Apple OS version 8.6 or later

USING THE CD WITH WINDOWS

To view the items located on the CD, follow these steps:

1. Insert the CD into your computer's CD-ROM drive.

2. A window appears with the following options:

Contents: Allows you to view the files included on the CD-ROM.

Software: Allows you to install useful software from the CD-ROM.

Links: Displays a hyperlinked page of websites.

Author: Displays a page with information about the Author(s).

Contact Us: Displays a page with information on contacting the publisher or author.

Help: Displays a page with information on using the CD.

Exit: Closes the interface window.

If you do not have autorun enabled, or if the autorun window does not appear, follow these steps to access the CD:

1. Click Start -> Run.

2. In the dialog box that appears, type d:<\\>start.exe, where d is the letter of your CD-ROM drive. This brings up the autorun window described in the preceding set of steps.

3. Choose the desired option from the menu. (See Step 2 in the preceding list for a description of these options.)

● ●

IN CASE OF TROUBLE

If you experience difficulty using the CD-ROM, please follow these steps:

1. Make sure your hardware and systems configurations conform to the systems requirements noted under "System Requirements" above.

2. Review the installation procedure for your type of hardware and operating system.

It is possible to reinstall the software if necessary.

To speak with someone in Product Technical Support, call 800–762–2974 or 317–572–3994 M–F 8:30 a.m. – 5:00 p.m. EST. You can also get support and contact Product Technical Support through our website at www.wiley. com/ techsupport.

Before calling or writing, please have the following information available:

● Type of computer and operating system

● Any error messages displayed

● Complete description of the problem.

It is best if you are sitting at your computer when making the call.

Pfeiffer Publications Guide

This guide is designed to familiarize you with the various types of Pfeiffer publications. The formats section describes the various types of products that we publish; the methodologies section describes the many different ways that content might be provided within a product. We also provide a list of the topic areas in which we publish.

FORMATS

In addition to its extensive book-publishing program, Pfeiffer offers content in an array of formats, from fieldbooks for the practitioner to complete, ready-to-use training packages that support group learning.

FIELDBOOK Designed to provide information and guidance to practitioners in the midst of action. Most fieldbooks are companions to another, sometimes earlier, work, from which its ideas are derived; the fieldbook makes practical what was theoretical in the original text. Fieldbooks can certainly be read from cover to cover. More likely, though, you'll find yourself bouncing around following a particular theme, or dipping in as the mood, and the situation, dictate.

HANDBOOK A contributed volume of work on a single topic, comprising an eclectic mix of ideas, case studies, and best practices sourced by practitioners and experts in the field.

An editor or team of editors usually is appointed to seek out contributors and to evaluate content for relevance to the topic. Think of a handbook not as a ready-to-eat meal, but as a cookbook of ingredients that enables you to create the most fitting experience for the occasion.

RESOURCE Materials designed to support group learning. They come in many forms: a complete, ready-to-use exercise (such as a game); a comprehensive resource on one topic (such as conflict management) containing a variety of methods and approaches; or a collection of like-minded activities (such as icebreakers) on multiple subjects and situations.

TRAINING PACKAGE An entire, ready-to-use learning program that focuses on a particular topic or skill. All packages comprise a guide for the facilitator/trainer and a workbook for the participants. Some packages are supported with additional media—such as video—or learning aids, instruments, or other devices to help participants understand concepts or practice and develop skills.

- *Facilitator/trainer's guide* Contains an introduction to the program, advice on how to organize and facilitate the learning event, and step-by-step instructor notes. The guide also contains copies of presentation materials—handouts, presentations, and overhead designs, for example—used in the program.

- *Participant's workbook* Contains exercises and reading materials that support the learning goal and serves as a valuable reference and support guide for participants in the weeks and months that follow the learning event. Typically, each participant will require his or her own workbook.

ELECTRONIC CD-ROMs and web-based products transform static Pfeiffer content into dynamic, interactive experiences. Designed to take advantage of the searchability, automation, and ease-of-use that technology provides, our e-products bring convenience and immediate accessibility to your workspace.

METHODOLOGIES

CASE STUDY A presentation, in narrative form, of an actual event that has occurred inside an organization. Case studies are not prescriptive, nor are they used to prove a point; they are designed to develop critical analysis and decision-making skills. A case study has a specific time frame, specifies a sequence of events, is narrative in structure, and contains a plot structure—an issue (what should be/have been done?). Use case studies when the goal is to enable participants to apply previously learned theories to the circumstances in the case, decide what is pertinent, identify the real issues, decide what should have been done, and develop a plan of action.

ENERGIZER A short activity that develops readiness for the next session or learning event. Energizers are most commonly used after a break or lunch to stimulate or refocus the group. Many involve some form of physical activity, so they are a useful way to counter post-lunch lethargy. Other uses include transitioning from one topic to another, where "mental" distancing is important.

EXPERIENTIAL LEARNING ACTIVITY (ELA) A facilitator-led intervention that moves participants through the learning cycle from experience to application (also known as a Structured Experience). ELAs are carefully thought-out designs in which there is a definite learning purpose and intended outcome. Each step—everything that participants do during the activity—facilitates the accomplishment of the stated goal. Each ELA includes complete instructions for facilitating the intervention and a clear statement of goals, suggested group size and timing, materials required, an explanation of the process, and, where appropriate, possible variations to the activity. (For more detail on Experiential Learning Activities, see the Introduction to the *Reference Guide to Handbooks and Annuals*, 1999 edition, Pfeiffer, San Francisco.)

GAME A group activity that has the purpose of fostering team spirit and togetherness in addition to the achievement of a pre-stated goal. Usually contrived—undertaking a desert expedition, for example—this type of learning method offers an engaging means for participants to demonstrate and practice business and interpersonal skills. Games are effective for team building and personal development mainly because the goal is subordinate to the process—the means through which participants reach decisions, collaborate, communicate, and generate trust and understanding. Games often engage teams in "friendly" competition.

ICEBREAKER A (usually) short activity designed to help participants overcome initial anxiety in a training session and/or to acquaint the participants with one another. An icebreaker can be a fun activity or can be tied to specific topics or training goals. While a useful tool in itself, the icebreaker comes into its own in situations where tension or resistance exists within a group.

INSTRUMENT A device used to assess, appraise, evaluate, describe, classify, and summarize various aspects of human behavior. The term used to describe an instrument depends primarily on its format and purpose. These terms include survey, questionnaire, inventory, diagnostic, survey, and poll. Some uses of instruments include providing instrumental feedback to group members, studying here-and-now processes or functioning within a group, manipulating group composition, and evaluating outcomes of training and other interventions.

Instruments are popular in the training and HR field because, in general, more growth can occur if an individual is provided with a method for focusing specifically on his or her own behavior. Instruments also are used to obtain information that will serve as a basis for change and to assist in workforce planning efforts.

Paper-and-pencil tests still dominate the instrument landscape with a typical package comprising a facilitator's guide, which offers advice on administering the instrument and interpreting the collected data, and an initial set of instruments. Additional instruments are available separately. Pfeiffer, though, is investing heavily in e-instruments. Electronic instrumentation provides effortless distribution and, for larger groups particularly, offers advantages over paper-and-pencil tests in the time it takes to analyze data and provide feedback.

LECTURETTE   A short talk that provides an explanation of a principle, model, or process that is pertinent to the participants' current learning needs. A lecturette is intended to establish a common language bond between the trainer and the participants by providing a mutual frame of reference. Use a lecturette as an introduction to a group activity or event, as an interjection during an event, or as a handout.

MODEL   A graphic depiction of a system or process and the relationship among its elements. Models provide a frame of reference and something more tangible, and more easily remembered, than a verbal explanation. They also give participants something to "go on," enabling them to track their own progress as they experience the dynamics, processes, and relationships being depicted in the model.

ROLE PLAY   A technique in which people assume a role in a situation/ scenario: a customer service rep in an angry-customer exchange, for example. The way in which the role is approached is then discussed and feedback is offered. The role play is often repeated using a different approach and/or incorporating changes made based on feedback received. In other words, role playing is a spontaneous interaction involving realistic behavior under artificial (and safe) conditions.

SIMULATION   A methodology for understanding the interrelationships among components of a system or process. Simulations differ from games in that they test or use a model that depicts or mirrors some aspect of reality in form, if not necessarily in content. Learning occurs by studying the effects of change on one or more factors of the model. Simulations are commonly used to test hypotheses about what happens in a system—often referred to as "what if?" analysis—or to examine best-case/worst-case scenarios.

THEORY   A presentation of an idea from a conjectural perspective. Theories are useful because they encourage us to examine behavior and phenomena through a different lens.

TOPICS

The twin goals of providing effective and practical solutions for workforce training and organization development and meeting the educational needs of training and human resource professionals shape Pfeiffer's publishing program. Core topics include the following:

Leadership & Management

Communication & Presentation

Coaching & Mentoring

Training & Development

E-Learning

Teams & Collaboration

OD & Strategic Planning

Human Resources

Consulting

What will you find on pfeiffer.com?

- The best in workplace performance solutions for training and HR professionals
- Downloadable training tools, exercises, and content
- Web-exclusive offers
- Training tips, articles, and news
- Seamless on-line ordering
- Author guidelines, information on becoming a Pfeiffer Affiliate, and much more

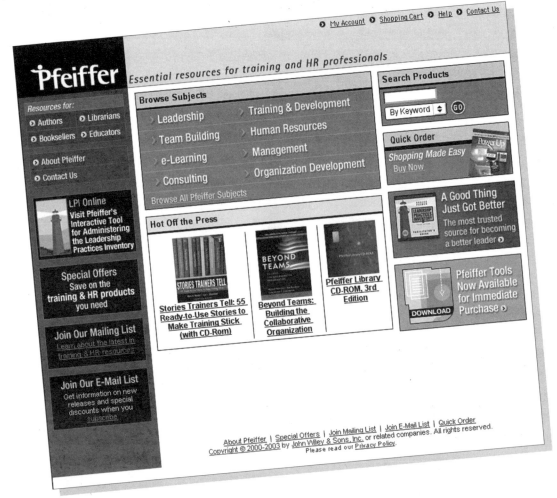

Discover more at www.pfeiffer.com

Learn-o-grams™